FUCK
IT'S
PAUL CANNELL

ME PLAYIN' FOR THE TOON

Published in Great Britain
by Poodle Publishing 2012

A CIP catalogue record for this book
is available from the British Library

ISBN 978-1475020793

Poodle Publishing
c/o 43 Queen Alexandra Rd. West
North Shields
NE29 9AA
Great Britain

© Cover designed by Paul Cannell

The Author

He used to be a professional footballer in the 70's and the 80's, not great, but not bad either. The Geordies would call him a 'canny' player. You may have heard of him not because of his footballing prowess, but because of his 'name'. 'Fuckin Hell, it's Paul Cannell' the phrase first coined by Brummie comic genius Jasper Carrott has followed him for the thirty odd years since he left Newcastle United where he enjoyed seven fantastic years. He did receive some respite from it during the four years he played in the North American Soccer League with teams such as the Washington Diplomats, the Memphis Rogues, the Calgary Boomers, and the Detroit Express, however on his return to the Toon, it started all over again; not on the terraces but in the bars, taxis, buses... even in the fuckin' butchers!

This book is a collection of controversial stories featuring some of the world's 'greats' such as Johann Cruyff, Malcolm Macdonald and Pele; some of the famous such as Howard Stern, President's daughter Susan Ford, Jerry Lee Lewis, Jasper Carrott and even fuckin' Sting and others such as his mates, Jimmy Steele and Bob Stetler, his drug dealer Joe and the infamous 'Memphis cookie man'. Oh, and I nearly forgot, there are some fuckin' twats in it as well... like Jimmy Hill the ex Coventry chairman and disgraced owner of the Detroit Express and the Washington Diplomats.

"It's a little bit chronological in that I've split it into three sections; my time in England, my time in the States and my time after football. The stories are about things that happened during my time in the game. Some are hilarious, some are surprising, some are shocking and some are disgusting. Some however, are hilariously, surprisingly, shockingly fuckin' disgusting... The stories you don't normally read about!"

DEDICATIONS

I've been told that I need to do a page of dedications; I asked why and was told you just do! There have been so many people who have affected or influenced me life. Far too many to list meaningfully here, so the criteria I have used is to list the people who, if given the opportunity, I would like to have another pint with..

Bill Shaw aka 'Billie the Pie'. Bill was my Bessie mate at school and during my time playing for The Toon. I only really lost touch with him when I moved to the States. I tried like hell to get him over there, but his fear of flying prevented that; "Planes, they're just flying Bombs" he would always say. 'Billy the Pie' stories are legendary, far too many to pick one out. It's sufficed to say that, if there is a 'big pub in the sky', Billy will be in there, keeping the regulars in stitches and drinking the bar dry! Cheers Billie.

Bob Stetler or Stetz... A team-mate at both the Washington Diplomats and the Memphis Rogues. I thought the world of Stetz. He was as mad as a hatter ... nothing fazed him or scared him. He was a true American gentleman and a right good lookin' bastard! Without a doubt, he'll be pullin' all the women in the 'big pub in the sky'.

Harry Storey... A schoolmate who I played football and cricket with for many years. 'Stogsy' became a very astute businessman who confounded the theory that you had to be mean and self centred to be a success. He'll be diffusing any altercations in the 'big pub in the sky!'

Me dad, Tony Cannell... Without a doubt he'll be in there drinking a pint of 'mixed' expounding his theories of space and time travel. At least he fulfilled his lifetime dream of sitting in a spaceship that had been to the moon. Mind you, the security staff at the Smithsonian were not too happy about it!

Me mother, Olwen... She'll be in the 'big pub in the sky' suppin' her Carlsberg Special Brew wondering why she feels tiddly and generally spoiling Tony's night! She'll leave before him and then the dog, Blitzen, will take her for a walk!

Davy Hall... Those who knew Davy will know that he's keeping the 'big pub in the sky's' punters entertained. Like the others on this page, he loved a pint almost as much as everyone loved him! I wish I'd known him longer...

I raise a glass to you all.

INTRODUCTION

So why is Paul Cannell age 58, who started playing football on the Spinney with the much older, infamous, Spinney Gang, now writing a book? Well, as I was often reminded by two great friends of mine Ken and John Somerville that I did play for one of the greatest football teams in Europe for a number of seasons; then travelled to America to play with and against some of the greatest players the world has ever seen at the height of the North American Soccer League. It took other people to make me realise that I had a story to tell.

I've written this book meself; nee ghost writers; If you spot any spelling mistakes or grammatical errors, then blame Bill Gates' Microsoft spell check or Heaton Grammar Schools' Dan Matthews who was my form teacher as well as my English Language teacher for my formative years. He also ran the school football team during the time I played for both the Northumberland and England Schoolboy teams. To me, colons and semi colons should have been taught in biology and not in English language lessons. I also might spell Terry Hibbitt with a smile or call Malcolm Macdonald" Ronald" a couple of times but so what, the stories are arl still the same.

I suppose I should apologise up front to my kids Ally and Ross for some of the things they're going to find out their dad got up to; but shit, everyone's got history otherwise they wouldn't have the phrase "do as I say, not as I do"

I hope you find these stories interesting and entertaining, I think you will cos', as Ken Somerville always said to me, "It's better to be a 'has been' than a 'never been'!!!"

ME PLAYIN'FOR THE DIPS

CONTENTS

PART ONE

FUCKIN'HELL IT'S PAUL CANNELL

PART TWO

STAR SPANGLED SOCCER, MY PART IN ITS DOWNFALL

PART THREE

COMING BACK TO MY ROOTS

1

ONCE A MACKEM, NOT ALWAYS A MACKEM!

My journey to signing for Newcastle United was a complicated one. During my time at Heaton Grammar school, I was selected to play for Newcastle Boys, Northumberland Boys and finally for England School Boys (where I had the dubious honour of being the first player ever, to be sent off. Well, it was against Scotland!).

Whilst at Heaton Grammar, I was playing regularly for Montague and North Fenham Boys Club. After scoring all six goals in a Boys Club final, I was approached by the head scout of Sunderland, Charlie Ferguson. He convinced me that I had the ability to become a professional footballer and so, consequently, I started playing on a regular basis for their team in the Northern intermediate league, along with the likes of Dennis Tueart, Richie Pitt and Derek Forster. Alan 'Bomber' Brown was Sunderland's manager at the time and he suggested that I needed toughening up. He arranged for me to sign for Whitley Bay so that I could play in the Northern League alongside a very experienced striker called Billy Wright, now sadly deceased. Billy was a good few years older than me and very experienced in the rough Northern League.

Just before we left the dressing room on my Whitley Bay debut, Billy took me to one side and said, "Paul, divven't worry about a thing, I'll look after you. When their keeper tries to kick the ball up the field out of his hands, just pick up the pieces." I didn't really know what he meant but, with the game only ten minutes old, their goalkeeper went to drop kick the ball out of his hands when Billy thrust his huge chest in the way; the ball hit him, he absorbed the impact and the ball dropped at my feet in front of an open goal. My first goal in the Northern League. I never had any hassle when playing for Whitley Bay!

After a couple of years playing for Sunderland, during which time I had never signed any schoolboy forms, we were due to play against Newcastle United. For some reason Alan Brown told me that I had to sign schoolboy forms in order to play against them, a game that I was obviously keen to play in. I was assured that it was simply a technicality and that if, at any time, I wanted to leave Sunderland, it would be no problem; so I signed the form. When the team sheet for the game went up, I was gutted to see that I hadn't been selected.

FUCKIN' HELL IT'S PAUL CANNELL

After the game, Joe Harvey and his coach, former Newcastle winger Geoff Allen, knocked on the door of me mam and dad's house. They explained to me that they had been watching me over a long period of time, Sunderland had found out and that is why they had made me sign the schoolboy forms and it was the reason they had not selected me to play in the game. They said that they wanted me to sign for the Toon when I finished my A levels. I however, was intending to go to Durham University to study law. Gentleman Joe used his great tact and explained "If you go to university and study law, you'll always wonder if you could have been a professional footballer. Sign for us, if Sunderland will release you, and if you don't make the grade you can always go back to university! Your salary will be £30 a week." Wowzers!

AN APPREHENSIVE LOOKING "ME" BEFORE ME ENGLAND SCHOOLBOY DEBUT
1971

I went training with Sunderland on the following Tuesday night, went into Alan Brown's office at the Washington training ground and asked him for my release. To his credit, he was as good as his word, apologised for the 'mix up' as he put it and that was it; I was on my way to St James' Park. I actually signed for

Newcastle at the same time as my mate, goalkeeper Eric Steele, who had played alongside me for Northumberland and England Schoolboys.

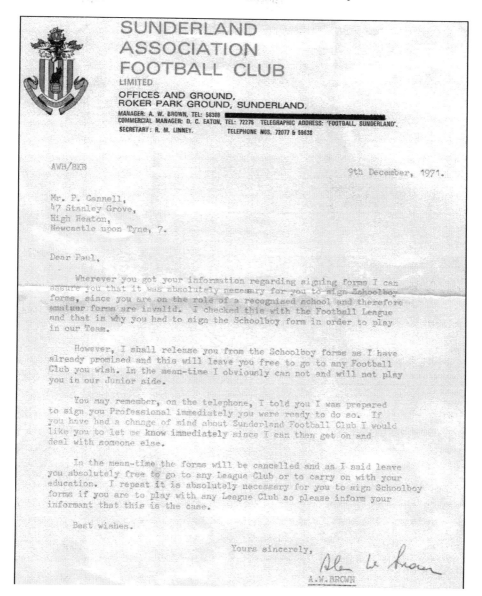

SUNDERLAND ASSOCIATION FOOTBALL CLUB LIMITED

OFFICES AND GROUND,
ROKER PARK GROUND, SUNDERLAND.

MANAGER: A. W. BROWN, TEL: 58308
COMMERCIAL MANAGER: D. C. EATON, TEL: 72275 TELEGRAPHIC ADDRESS: 'FOOTBALL, SUNDERLAND'.
SECRETARY: R. M. LINNEY. TELEPHONE NOS. 72077 & 58638

AWB/BKB

9th December, 1971.

Mr. P. Cannell,
47 Stanley Grove,
High Heaton,
Newcastle upon Tyne, 7.

Dear Paul,

Wherever you got your information regarding signing forms I can assure you that it was absolutely necessary for you to sign Schoolboy forms, since you are on the role of a recognised school and therefore amateur forms are invalid. I checked this with the Football League and that is why you had to sign the Schoolboy form in order to play in our Team.

However, I shall release you from the Schoolboy forms as I have already promised and this will leave you free to go to any Football Club you wish. In the mean-time I obviously can not and will not play you in our Junior side.

You may remember, on the telephone, I told you I was prepared to sign you Professional immediately you were ready to do so. If you have had a change of mind about Sunderland Football Club I would like you to let me know immediately since I can then get on and deal with someone else.

In the mean-time the forms will be cancelled and as I said leave you absolutely free to go to any League Club or to carry on with your education. I repeat it is absolutely necessary for you to sign Schoolboy forms if you are to play with any League Club so please inform your informant that this is the case.

Best wishes.

Yours sincerely,

A.W. BROWN

THE LETTER THAT LET ME LEAVE THE MACKEMS TO JOIN THE TOON 1971

2

GENTLEMAN JOE

Joe Harvey was the manager who persuaded me to sign for Newcastle United and not for Sunderland. Gentleman Joe was a wonderful man who lived for the fans, the club and for his golf! He could never be accused of being tactically astute, but his man management skills were on par with the likes of Manchester United's Alex Ferguson. One particular event stands out in my mind.

Smoking was a habit not recommended for professional athletes, but two of the Toon's greatest players, Malcolm McDonald and Terry Hibbitt were twenty a day men. As soon as the half time whistle blew, they were first down the tunnel and into the dressing room sparking up! Our coach at the time was Keith Burkinshaw, (who went on to become a very successful manager at Spurs) and he didn't approve of the dressing room smoke-in. Keith expressed his disapproval of smoking in general but especially smoking in the home team dressing room. After numerous requests for the two main perpetrators to quit smoking, he eventually convinced the gaffer, gentleman Joe, to pass an edict... NO SMOKING IN THE DRESSING ROOM! The law was passed, the players informed and a sign was strategically placed above the dressing room door for all to see. It read:

NO SMOKING IN THE DRESSING ROOM
JOE HARVEY
MANAGER

The next game was on a Wednesday night. I was substitute and when the half time whistle blew, Malcolm and Terry sprinted down the tunnel and sparked up. Burky immediately snapped "Put those filthy tabs out, can you not see the fuckin' sign?" All hell broke loose with Mal and Terry refusing to obey, threatening to leave the club if they couldn't have a cigarette. In the midst of this half time mayhem, Joe Harvey sauntered into the dressing room with the usual cup of tea in his hand and, in his typically laid back way, he inquired what the problem was, after all we were winning 2-0. Burky explained the situation citing lack of respect, disobedience and rebellion (as well as a few more choice expletives). Mal and Terry just dug their heels in further and threatened not to come out for the second half. Joe casually put his cup of tea down, disappeared into the adjoining treatment room and returned with a felt tipped pen. He pulled up a chair under the offending sign, stood up on it and wrote an addendum to the sign. It then read:

NO SMOKING IN THE DRESSING ROOM
JOE HARVEY
MANAGER
EXCEPT TERRY HIBBITT AND MALCOLM McDONALD

Problem solved!

Another good example of Joe Harvey's man management technique was when I decided to go in and ask for a pay rise. I'd been on £30 a week for a couple of seasons but had just started to get the occasional game for the first team and had been scoring fairly regularly.

I booked an appointment to see Joe as my contract was coming up for renewal. I knocked on his office door just after training and was welcomed in warmly. He was sat behind his desk, listening to the radio (or it could have been the greyhound racing) and drinking a cup of tea. The conversation went a bit like this:

Me – "Boss"

Joe – "Hang on son; you went to Benidorm in the summer didn't you?"

Me – "Yes"

Joe – "Where did you stay?"

Me – "The Rosamar"

Joe – "The Rosamar, that's the big high rise just behind the Don Pancho isn't it?"

Me – "Yes"

Joe – "What's it like in there?"

I explained the pros and cons of staying at the Rosamar, its location, entertainment, food, pool etc.

Joe – "Me and the wife stayed at the Bristol Park, we've been going there for years but I feel that the standard has been slipping lately"

Me – "Well I would definitely recommend the Rosamar, it's..."

And so it went on. After about twenty minutes I shook his hand, left the office and was quite looking forward to my next Benidorm holiday. I'd totally forgotten what I'd gone in to see him about! Crafty bastard! Naturally, Joe and his wife continued to stay at the Bristol Park for years!!!!

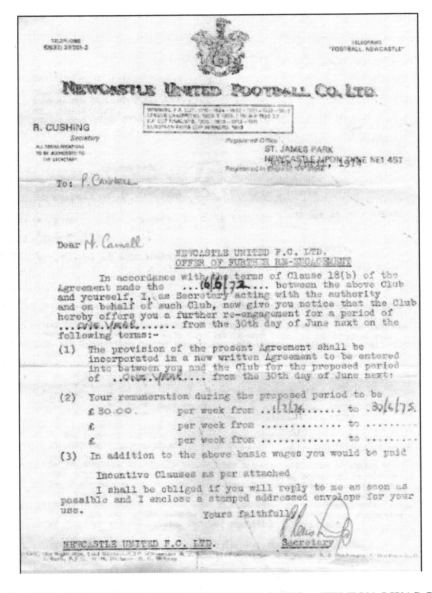

CONTRACTS WERE GEET SIMPLE IN THOSE DAYS... TELT YA I WAS ONLY GETTING' 30 QUID A WEEK!!!

3

IN SAFE HANDS... I DIVVEN'T THINK SO!

Alec Mutch and Benny Craig were the physios for Newcastle United in the 70's, two great blokes, but without a huge amount of medical training. I wish I had a pound for every time I heard them use the phrase "run it off".

I once left Malcolm McDonald on the treatment table at about 10am, went training and returned back to St. James' Park around 1pm. Mal was still on the treatment table. "What are you doing still lying there?" I asked him. "They want to give me as much heat as possible on my knee to get me fit for the weekend" replied Mal. "Well if I was you, I would have read a book because they've got a bloody reading lamp on your leg instead of a heat lamp" I informed him.

After the dreadful Bradford City fire that killed so many supporters, new laws were being imposed on all clubs that had wooden stands (as was Newcastle's "Old Stand"). One of the stipulations was that the fire brigade, in the event of a fire, had to have access to a specific amount of water within a certain pumping distance of the ground. Newcastle were in trouble as, no matter how hard they tried, the fire brigade simply could not access the amount of water needed to comply with the new regulations. Time and time again they tried but to no avail. Step forward Mutchy...

Years ago, in the 50's, Newcastle, seemingly, had their own swimming pool. Where was it now? It was under the treatment room floor. They'd deemed it unhygienic and built over it. After a cursory inspection to confirm its dimensions, it was calculated that it could hold sufficient water to satisfy the new regulations! To my knowledge no water was ever put into the pool and even if it was, in the event of a fire, they would have had to rip up the treatment room floor to gain access to the water!

As I said, treatment was pretty basic, ultrasound, infrared and hot and cold water with ice. After home games, injured players had to report to the treatment room to have their injuries checked by the club doctor.

Frank Clark had been injured in a bizarre incident where he 'tackled' the corner flag which snapped and impaled his leg leaving a nasty deep wound (this was when corner flags were made of wood). Dr Salkeld, the club doctor, was concerned that, after a few weeks, the wound showed no signs of healing. "Well, just keep on cleaning the wound and putting the penicillin powder on it and we'll check it out next week". Frank looked daggers at Mutchy. He'd never seen any penicillin powder at all; no bloody wonder the wound wasn't healing! Pills were given out like sweets at Newcastle, an envelope full of penicillin for infections and a handful of red, round tablets for swellings to muscles and joints. When, out of curiosity, I asked what these red pills actually were, I was told that they were Butazoladene or 'Bute', a drug that was illegal to give to a horse, but absolutely fine to give to a professional footballer!

Another time the scary side of the medical regime at Newcastle surfaced was after a particular home game. John Bird had damaged his teeth, one missing and another very slack. He was upset that no dental appointment had been made for over a week and the slack tooth was causing him some pain. I watched the club doctor go into the back room and get a tooth extractor, hide it behind his back and go to see Birdie who was sitting on a low seat. The doctor bent over and asked which the offending tooth was; he then produced the extractor and quickly yanked the slack tooth out. Birdie was in agony, he recoiled and kicked the doctor in the balls which made him screech out some choice language then roll around the floor whilst blood poured from Birdie's mouth. Those were the days; who needs Carry On Doctor?

The worst example of medical malpractice occurred every season when the players received their flu jabs. We queued in an orderly, if somewhat nervous, line in the treatment room as the doctor injected the players one by one. However it was not like it is today, with a new sterile needle, syringe and a measured dose for each player. It was one big syringe that only got changed when it became blunt, which was usually after about five players and the dosage was measured by eye!!! Just as well aids wasn't around in those days and the nastiest thing that the players caught was the pox!

4

ALL WHITE NOW

To say that things were run professionally back in the 70's would totally be takin' the piss... as this next tale explains.

We were playing Birmingham City, on a cold winter Wednesday evening, in a cup tie. Snow had been forecast however, by the 7.30 kick off time, the pitch was hard, but no snow had fallen. I can't remember the score line at the time but, with about fifteen minutes to go until half time, the heavens suddenly opened. Thick white snowflakes tumbled onto the St. James' pitch, accumulating rapidly. As it was really cold, the snow remained powdery so it didn't interfere with the movement of the ball across the pitch and so the referee allowed play to continue. With about a minute to go before the referee blew his whistle for half time, our goal keeper, Mick Mahoney, drop-kicked the ball out of his hands aiming for us, his forwards. The white Mitre Multiplex ball landed on the pitch somewhere in the Birmingham City half of the field and, for a full thirty seconds, twenty two footballers and a referee were looking for a ball that had totally disappeared... like something from the fuckin' X Files !

The ball was eventually found nestled in a pile of snow near the old paddock side of the ground ten yards from the Leazes End touchline. The referee, realising the situation, blew for half time and the teams headed for the warmth of the dressing rooms.

As we were enjoying a welcome cup of tea in the dressing room, the referee entered and asked, no ordered, us to change the white ball for an orange one to enable the second half to continue. Alec Mutch the 'physio' whose job it was, for some reason, to have the match balls prepared, explained that he didn't have an orange ball even though snow had been forecast all bloody week! Not a problem; Stan Seymour, the club chairman, owned a sports shop in the centre of Newcastle and it was he who supplied the clubs' footballs. Ray Hudson, an apprentice at the time, was given the shop keys and told to run down to the sports shop and bring back an orange ball. A super fit Rocky raced down to Seymour Sports, got an orange ball and then legged it back to St James'. The ball was duly inflated and made it onto the park for the second half that had only been delayed for a couple of minutes. By the end of the game, an invoice for the ball was left lying, by Stan Seymour, on the physiotherapist's treatment bed!

Speakin' of Ray Hudson, he like meself ended up in America. When I returned to the Toon after my loan spell with the Washington Diplomats 'Rocky' was the first in me face to ask iz' what it was like. "Fabulous", I told him; then set about recounting tales of sex and drugs n' rock and football!

Rocky was very like meself, a young local lad that was struggling to get the break into the first team. He was magic on the ball but he was, and I'm sure he'll not mind me saying this, a bit daft! I tried to convince him that if he got the chance he'd be mad not to give it a go over the ocean. Well fuck me, who was playing for The Fort Lauderdale Strikers in one of my first games for the Dips on my return to the N.A.S.L. aye….Rocky, alongside several world class players …. And he was the best player on the park! He was so excited about his life that I could hardly understand him; not because he'd picked up an American accent but because his high pitched Geordie accent had got worse!

Unlike meself, Rocky has made his home in the States and is now a 'famous' soccer commentator on some Spanish channel over there; they love his Geordie accent and they reckon he's still daft as the proverbial brush!

RAY 'ROCKY' HUDSON

5

PRE MATCH WARM UP

Drinking was an acceptable part of football in the 70's; however, even then, it was an absolute no-no on match days.

We were playing a League Cup game, at home, on a Wednesday night. As usual, the squad had to report to the ground an hour and a half before kick off. Although a list of players had been displayed on the notice board in the dressing room; the actual team had not yet been announced. This was the norm; the actual team would go up an hour before kick off when the team sheets had to be handed in to the referee. Everyone was in the dressing room, the players, Keith Burkinshaw the coach, the physios (lol) and Joe Harvey the manager. Joe was just about to put the team sheet on the notice board when he realised that one of the players due to play that night, was missing. Minutes ticked by and still the player was a no show. It was an hour until kick off and the team sheets were due to go to the referee. Joe had to make a decision; should he take the missing player (one of United's greats) off the team sheet completely or relegate him to substitute in the hope that he would turn up. I was due to be substitute (in the days of only one substitute) and so if the boss decided on the latter option I was going to be in the starting eleven. He chose the latter and so, all of a sudden, I was playing that evening... however it meant we had no substitute unless the missing player turned up.

It got to approximately seven o'clock, half an hour until kick off, before the missing player stumbled through the door, obviously under the influence. Just as he was about to be bollocked by Burkinshaw, Joe Harvey intervened. "We'll sort this out later, get changed you're still sub"!

We took to the field with the subdued sub in the dugout. The first half started and our sub snoozed, quite oblivious to what was happening on the field of play. Unfortunately, after thirty minutes or so, one of the starting eleven got injured and had to leave the pitch. I'll always remember the coaching staff having to shake our sub to wake him up and almost push him onto the pitch. We all knew what had happened previously and we were wondering what our sub could contribute to the game. We needn't have worried; he played a blinder, possibly his best performance in a United shirt and we left the field victorious with the crowd none the wiser but still perhaps, wondering why one of our star players had been made substitute.

P.S. I have not named the player because he was one of my heroes!

I HOPE SOME FUCKER DOESN'T GET INJURED...

6

FUCKIN' HELL IT'S PAUL CANNELL!

My parents must have had a sense of humour when they named me Paul. I'd never realised its comic implication until I had lunch with the Brummie comedian Jasper Carrott.

I'd been down to London with a few of the Newcastle players, to attend the professional footballer's awards dinner and the evening's entertainment was a gentleman called Jasper Carrott, who we'd never heard of; the only thing we'd been told was that he was supposed to be big in the Midlands. Anyway, during his spot, Malcolm McDonald and I cried with laughter for an hour and a half and so we were delighted that, when he had finished, he joined us for several bevvies. Malcolm and I were on Frank Clark's testimonial committee and it was our job to put on shows to raise money for the fund. Jasper said he'd be more than happy to come up to Newcastle to do a show for Frank; it would help his career, as he was virtually unknown in the North East.

Once back in Newcastle, Malcolm and I got on with the job in hand. We got the media interested, booked the City Hall and started selling tickets. We rang Jasper and confirmed the date of the concert and agreed to meet him, at lunchtime on the day of the show, at St James' Park.

By the time of the concert, we'd sold around a thousand tickets which, although it wouldn't fill the City Hall, made us feel pretty good considering the punters had never really heard of Jasper Carrott; they were coming simply because they were Newcastle United fans.

Jasper arrived at St James' Park just after we had finished training. Malcolm and I jumped into his Jag and drove to Jim & Carole's Kitchen on Blenheim Street, Newcastle, about a quarter of a mile from the Park.

When we arrived, the restaurant was totally empty. The Maître De asked us if we had a reservation which caused Carrott to burst into uncontrollable laughter, looking at all the empty tables. Jim and Carole, who had run the Astor Club, Roy's Two Rooms and Jim's Kitchen (all great restaurants) joined us and after many 'aperitifs' Jasper exclaimed "What the Por Cannell is going on here!". We all looked at him in surprise. "How can you have a name like Por

Cannell?" he continued "It's the ideal swear word". Well I'd never thought about it before but, after Jasper highlighted it, it suddenly struck me that I'd lived with this name for twenty plus years and it had taken a Brummie comic to point out the obvious. My parents, the twats, I think they already knew!

After a few more bevvies, we were all feeling quite 'happy' and now I was Por Cannell, not plain old Paul Cannell. We left the restaurant and got into Jasper's car where he immediately donned a chauffeur's cap, which he wore backwards as we sped off to St James' Park. Suddenly, and without warning, just as we got outside the Scottish & Newcastle Brewery (which used to lie in the shadow of St. James' Park), he pulled up alongside a startled pedestrian, wound the window down and asked him how to get to where Newcastle United played. The guy looked through the cars open window and exclaimed "Bloody hell you're Malcolm McDonald, oh and you're Paul Cannell, will yuz' sign me bus ticket?" He thrust a ticket into the car and Mal and I signed it. "You're bloody great Mal, the best centre forward the Toon has ever had!" Much to Carrott's amusement, he then went on to tell us how to get to St James' Park which we could actually see! The Geordies are magic!

FRANK CLARK AND JASPER CARROTT, FUCK KNOWS WHERE THE PHOTO WAS TAKEN. DON'T SAY IT, ONE OF THEM IS A COMEDIAN AND THE OTHER ONE IS A FOOTBALLER, BUT WHICH ONE?

FUCKIN' HELL IT'S PAUL CANNELL

Anyhoo, that night at the concert Jasper spent a good ten minutes, taking the piss out of my name which the audience, being Newcastle fans, absolutely loved, and Jasper brought the house down.

This was on the Thursday. On the Saturday I was starting in the first team and during the warm up period I was welcomed by the Leazes End choir with a huge chant of "Fuckin' hell, it's Paul Cannell", and it has never stopped, even to this day. In fact I was once in a pub in Coventry having a pint when someone missed an easy shot whilst playing pool "Por Cannell" he shouted!

The chant expanded when Gordon Lee sold Malcolm McDonald to Arsenal and I became the regular striker; "They sold McDonald for Cannell, doo dah, doo dah..." (To the tune of the Camp down Races) more pure Geordie genius! And even now thirty odd years later, people still come up to me and say "Eeh, can you remember all the times we shouted "Por Cannell!" I can walk into a random pub and have them chanting away; "Fuckin hell, it's Paul Cannell!" I wish I had a quid for every time I've heard this over the years cos' I'd be a rich man now, and not because of my football skills.

P.S. Jasper Carrott continued to feature this story in his live shows for a couple of years as he gained fame and notoriety and it even ended up on his successful first live album 'Carrott Live at Notts' as well as in his book 'A Little Zit On The Side'. Even comedian Harry Hill has used the 'swear-name' Por Cannell"!

7

MEGGY THOO

It was still Frank Clark's testimonial year. Frank loved rock n' roll music and was an accomplished guitarist. I thought it would be a canny idea to put a band together with him and call it 'The Frank Clark Band'.

At the time, I had a mobile disco and one of the DJs was a school friend of mine called Andy Green. Not only was he a brilliant DJ but an excellent singer. Another mate was a guy called Darco... Davy Darco, known to everyone in the music business to this day. A total eccentric, a genius and a genuinely lovely lad, and he also played a mean lead guitar. Playing bass guitar was another pal of mine, Dave McGibbon, also known as 'Funky'; he had played with The Delamares, a well known 60's chart band, but he was probably more famous for having been married to one of the Vernon girls. We found a drummer whose name escapes me, and then there was Clarky on rhythm guitar. We all got together and worked out a set of songs that we thought would go down well in the social clubs around the North East. I asked Frank if he felt up to actually singing a song, instead of just playing rhythm in the background. After all, the act was called The Frank Clark Band. Frank agreed and decided to sing his favourite song, Peggy Sue.

Our first rehearsal was arranged to take place in the Newton Park Hotel, a pub in Benton Newcastle, where a great mate of mine, Jack Watson, was the manager. We were booked in at 4pm as another band was using the room for their rehearsals. We arrived at about 3.45pm and watched this other band doing their thing. We had a natter amongst ourselves and the general consensus was that they were quite good. However when it got to 4.15pm and they were still playing, we started to get a bit pissed off. I nipped behind the bar and knocked on Jack's office door. "Jack" I moaned, "this band won't get off the stage so we're only going to get a couple of hours practice before you re-open" (this was at the time when pubs shut in the afternoon). Jack got up off his seat and stormed into the concert room. He ordered the band off the stage, informing them that the Frank Clark Band had the room booked from 4pm and that they were very important! They started packing up their gear, muttering and moaning to each other; showing obvious signs of displeasure. Once they had gone, I thanked Jack and asked him what they called the band that had just left, as I thought they were fuckin' good. "Oh that lot, they've been practising in here for ages" replied Jack. "They're called Last Exit, and the chappie at the front is called Gordon err... Sumner... I think".... STING!

LAST EXIT
WE HAD TO GET THIS LOT CHUCKED OFF THE STAGE... COZ' THE FRANK CLARK BAND HAD ARRIVED!

Anyway after an hour or so, it got to Frank's big moment, Peggy Sue! Well, if you know a bit about Frank Clark, you'll know that he has a slight speech impediment; his S's sound like Th's, and his P's sound like M's. So, much to our amusement, he broke into his very own rendition of "Meggy Thoo, Meggy Thoo, mitty mitty mitty mitty Meggy Thoo!" On review however, we decided to leave the song on the play list as, apart from the slightly original lyrics, he sang and played the song bloody well! It was a good decision, as the punters lapped it up in all the clubs. The Frank Clark Band went on to play around twelve gigs, raising money for the testimonial in pubs and clubs all over the North East from Walker in Newcastle to Lennie Hepple's Fandango night club in Hexham. Unfortunately, that bloody Gordon Sumner had more success and slightly more longevity!!! C'est las vie.

ME, STEWY' BARRACLOUGH,TONY BELL ALAN 'BUDGIE' KENNEDY AND FRANK CLARK.(FUCKIN' LEFT TO RIGHT!)

8

HOWZAT!

You wouldn't normally include a cricket match in a footballers testimonial year however Frank Clark loved his cricket, so did Malcolm McDonald and so did I … and Mal and I were organising Frank's testimonial events!

We decided to form two teams, one captained by a lad called Asif Masood, a Pakistani international who was a real character, the other by Frank Clark. I was a member of Asif's eleven, along with John Tudor, Irving Nattrass, Bobby Moncur (who was now playing for the Mackems) and Malcolm McDonald, the rest of our team was made up of local County cricketers. Frank's team consisted of David Mills, Alan Foggon and David Armstrong (all Middlesbrough) as well as Jimmy Montgomery and Bryan 'Pop' Robson who were playing for the 'scum' oops…I mean Sunderland, at the time; again, the rest of their team were County players. Asif was definitely 'larger than life'; he was a bowler whose run up had been described by John Arlott as akin to " Groucho Marx chasing a pretty waitress"…. and rendered his name Masif Asood! I was, and still am, a huge cricket fan so this event meant a lot to me.

The Jesmond County Cricket Ground was packed for the match. After an elongated warm up i.e. several dozen pints, the two teams took to the field, well our team did along with their two opening batsmen. Asif opened the bowling to roars of approval for his weird run up and bowling action. Then the applause reached new heights as local hero Malcolm McDonald took off his sweater to bowl the second over. Now I'd never seen Mal bowl before, I knew he could play a bit and I'd heard he was quite quick but I, along with the huge crowd were amazed at what we were about to see. He started his run up some thirty yards from the bowling crease, gradually accelerating… getting faster and faster as the roar of the crowd increased until, at the point of delivery, he was travelling at his Olympic qualifying speed. As the noise of the crowd reached a crescendo he released the ball, which was a bit on the short side; and he simply kept on running…… I swear to God, he passed the wicket keeper, Ken Pearson, before the fuckin' ball had passed the outside edge of the batsmen's bat!!!! I've seen nowt like it. The fans loved it, and so did I.

Obviously, when bowling like that, you don't have a long spell so, after a couple of overs, Asif asked me to warm up. I wasn't a bad cricketer, I'd played for the county whilst at school and, once I'd retired from professional football, I played for Kirkley in the Northumberland League. I suppose I'd call myself an all rounder....crap with bat and ball! Football wise, at the time, I was usually getting games in the first team when either John Tudor or Malcolm McDonald were injured - so it'll come as no surprise that it did cross my mind to set a field with Tudor at silly mid off and Mal at silly mid on and bowl a series of half volley's….. However common sense got the better of me and I set a traditional field. Anyhoo, we had a great day; I couldn't tell you who won but I don't think it mattered. We raised a fair amount of cash for the testimonial fund and we all got pissed!

```
Asif Masood - Frank Clark Testimonial - Asif Masood XI  V  Frank Clark XI
Played at Jesmond, Northumberland County Cricket Club Ground on Sunday 14th Sept

Asif Masood XI.                                                    Total.

  1. .Asif Masood **   County Club & Pakistan &North'd
  2. M.McDonald        Newcastle U.F.C. & England
  3. J.Tudor           Newcastle U.F.C.
  4. I.Nattrass        Newcastle U.F.C. & England Under 23
  5. P.Cannell         Newcastle U.F.C.
  6. W.Smalley         Benwell Hill & North'd
  7. J.Thewlis         County Club & North'd
  8. J.M.Crawhall      Morpeth & North'd
  9. R.Muncur          Sunderland UFC & Scotalnd
 10. W.G.Robson Ø      Alnwick & North'd
 11. K.Earl            County Club & North'd
                                        Extras

                                                  Total.

Fall of Wickets:  1/   2/   3/   4/   5/   6/   7/   8/   9/

Frank Clark XI.

  1. Frank Clark **    Ex Newcastle U.F.C.
  2. D.Mills           Middles'bro Engalnd Under 23
  3. A.Foggon          Middles'bro
  4. J.Montgomery      Sunderland
  5. B.Robson          Sunderland & England under 23
  6. A.A.Johnson       Whitburn CC & North'd
  7. A.Brown           Benwell & North'd
  8. A.S.Thompson      Benwell & North'd
  9. K.Pearson Ø       County Club & North'd
 10. A.Hardy           Percy Main & North'd
 11. D.Armstrong       Middles'bro & England under 23.
                                        Extras

                                                  Total

Fall of Wickets:  1/   2/   3/   4/   5/   6/   7/   8/   9/

Play commences at 2.30 PM.     Limited to 40 Overs per innings.

** Captain
Ø  Wicket Keeper            Admission by Scorecard: ............  50p.
                            Penizers & Children..............  25p

        PLEASE READ SCOREBOARD FOR CORRECT BATTING ORDER.
```

THE OFFICIAL SCORE CARD FOR CLARKY'S TESTIMONIAL CRICKET MATCH

FUCKIN' HELL IT'S PAUL CANNELL

While we're on the subject of cricket, as I said I played for Kirkley whose new captain was Bobby Tulip a friend of mine from school. He was keen to make an impact as the new skipper and had set about looking for some new players. By coincidence, John, a friend of mine rang me up to say that his sister had moved back to Newcastle with her new boyfriend who happened to be a 'canny cricketer' and he was looking for a local team to play with. I told him to tell his sister that we had nets the following night and that I'd pick him up and we'd see if he was any good.

GRAHAM ROOPE
SURREY, ENGLAND AND KIRKLEY

FUCKIN' HELL IT'S PAUL CANNELL

We drove to nets the following night and on the way I discovered that her boyfriend's name was Graham, he came from down south (which, to me, made him a Cockney) he'd played a fair bit of cricket but was also a keen goalkeeper and had played semi pro for several teams. Once we got to practice, I introduced him to Bobby who had a bit of a chat with him then asked him to get padded up. Graham sauntered to the strike end of the net then casually, elegantly and stylishly destroyed our bowlers." Where the fuck did you learn to bat like that?" I asked him when he'd finished his spell in the net "Surrey" he replied "and England." "Well what's your full name?" asked a bewildered Bobby "Graham Richard James Roope" he replied. Needless to say Bobby signed him for Kirkley!

9

TICKET TOUTS

There were many examples of impropriety involving Newcastle United's directors in the seventies but I tended to ignore them and on several occasions, I even defended them. That was until I was on the receiving end.

My best mate Billy the Pie was in London studying chiropody and I'd promised on several occasions to visit him. The F.A. Cup Final that year was between West Ham and Fulham so I decided that we might as well go to the game while I was down there. I didn't think tickets would be a problem as I knew all Football League clubs got an allocation and I didn't think many people from Newcastle would want to see a game that we had no real interest in. I asked Russell Cushing, the club secretary, if I could buy a couple of tickets. "No chance" said Russell, "we didn't get enough".

I decided to give a well-known ticket tout from Gateshead a call to see if he could help me out. "No problem" he replied "how many do you need?" I bought two tickets at five times their face value but what really pissed me off was that on the reverse of the tickets it had the official Newcastle United allocation stamp! I was livid and went straight to see Russell Cushing who apologised profusely and said he would look into it as a matter of urgency.

The following day, after training, Russell asked me to come into his office. When I got there I was met by club director Gordon McKeag. The tickets had been traced to him. He nervously explained to me that he had given the tickets to a 'friend 'of his, who without his 'knowledge' must have sold them to this ticket tout. Hmmm, a likely story…

10

PHANTOM UNITED

As I telt ye before (depending on which part of the book this story ends up!) Benidorm was our favourite end of season holiday destination; probably cos' it was all we could afford! This year, there was me, Alan Kennedy, Derek Craig, Davey Crosson and Billy Coulson, all staying at the Rosamar Hotel along with two mates of mine, Alan Moy and Dave McGibbon. Billy Coulson's nickname was Coco as he had the whitest, wildest hair you'd ever seen, which we blamed on his love of Pernod. On about the third day of our holiday we had a game of footy against the hotel's bartenders and waiters on a piece of waste land close to the hotel.

Dave McGibbon was a bit on the portly side and decided to sit the game out and have a cup of coffee in a cafe overlooking our makeshift pitch. He was joined by a well-dressed, Spanish gentleman who spoke very good English and was very impressed with our footballing prowess.

"They are very skilful" he said to Dave who replied "well they should be because it's Newcastle United". The Spaniard's eyes lit up, "Ooo, Newcastle United; would they like play against my team next Wednesday?"… Without knowing what the fuck he was getting us into Dave replied "Of course they would, what time?"

The game was organised for 3pm at Benidorm's football ground. Dave explained the situation to us but we forgot all about it until Jim Kennerly, the owner of the Big Ben Tavern, a popular bar in the centre of Benidorm, came to see us at the hotel holding up a large poster. We knew Jim very well as we had drunk in his pub for several years. "Do you lot realise that everyone thinks Newcastle United are playing Benidorm on Wednesday?" asked Jim, "Benidorm are a proper Spanish second division team, they're proper… real… do you know what you've got yourselves into? I've been trying to organise a game there for years and you've come away on bloody holiday and ended up with a game against Benidorm. Jesus, do you know they've sold two thousand tickets already? Hundreds of Geordies are expecting to see Newcastle United. How many players have you actually got?". "Ermm, about six" I replied sheepishly. "Right" said Jim, "I'll rustle up another five players. By the way, have you got a strip?" He knew that was a daft question… "Right" said Jim, "I'll sort that out as well".

There were posters all over the resort and cars with loudspeakers driving up and down the streets advertising the game. On the day of the match, we arrived at Benidorm's ground an hour before kick-off and Jim introduced us to our new team mates; Mervyn Day (West Ham) was our goalkeeper, Phil Boersma (Liverpool) was to play up front with me, two Germans (from some team in the Bundesliga) in central defence and Ray Graydon (Burnley) wide on the right. None of us had any boots, only trainers and no shin pads, but at least we did have a strip thanks to Jim.

BENIDORM'S FOOTY PITCH WHERE WOR PHANTOM UNITED WERE HELD TO A "DULL, BORING, GOALESS DRAW". TO MOST OF WOR TEAM, IT WAS WA FIRST GAME IN EUROPE!

At kick off, there was a crowd of around 2,200 all expecting a full Newcastle United team or so we thought; however the Spaniards were none the wiser and the Geordies were that drunk that they probably thought it was a home match on a hot day back in the Toon!

Anyway, the game ended in a goalless draw, Billy Coulson got hit on the head by a brick and got sent off for picking up the brick and chasing the kid who threw it. Then the Geordies started fighting with the Spanish spectators and the police had to move in. All this, together with the fact that most of our players were still suffering from gargantuan hangovers from the night before (well we did think we were on holiday), didn't make for the best performance... We declined the offer to attend an after game reception and legged it back to Jim Kennerly's Big Ben Tavern. We thought we'd just about blagged it, until the next day. The headlines in the regions English speaking newspaper the Costa Blanca News read; NEWCASTLE UNITED HELD TO A DULL GOALLESS DRAW BY BENIDORM!!!

When we returned home to England for pre-season training, our new manager Gordon Lee demanded to know how his 'new team' had played in Benidorm. We hadn't realised that John Gibson from the Evening Chronicle had already broken the story while we were still in Spain!

Once the season got underway, Joe Harvey, our ex boss, returned to St. James' Park to get some treatment on an injury he had sustained playing golf (his passion). When I bumped into him in the dressing room he told me he had been on holiday in Benidorm with his wife at the time of the phantom match. They had been walking to the beach when a van, fitted with loudspeakers, had passed by them broadcasting information about the match. It had made them stop in their tracks. "Are we going to go and watch the lads play?" his wife had asked; Joe seemingly burst out laughing as he knew that it was just us on holiday. Needless to say they didn't go!

11

IF I HAD A PHOTOGRAPH OF YOU

Our flight had just landed at Alicante Airport and we were all looking forward to our annual piss up in the sun; quite unaware of the uproar we were about to cause with our unscheduled game against Benidorm. Davey Crosson, Alan Kennedy, Billy Coulson and I had just passed through passport control, with the on duty officer having given our passports the usual cursory glance; this was a long time before any terrorist threats were perceived. Only one of our group had yet to clear the control, Derek Craig.

'Craigey' had signed for Newcastle around the same time as me; he was a big lad, even for a centre half, with a large Mexican style moustache and a big afro hairstyle that covered his slightly protruding ears. He was generally regarded, by the ladies and himself, as a bit of a looker; however none of us had ever seen his passport photograph! As we stood around waiting, I happened to look back to see him at the head of a long queue of arriving passengers, just approaching the passport control kiosk. Once there, he handed the lethargic officer his passport, open at the page that contained his photograph and waited, with his hand outstretched, for it to be returned. Manuel (we shall call him) actually looked at his photo, looked at Craigey's face then back at the photo. He proceeded to burst into incontrollable laughter and summoned the passport controllers from the other two kiosks that were on duty at the time, to have a look. All three of them were pointing at poor Derek's passport photograph then pointing and laughing at him. Even the passengers stuck in the queue were laughing, some even coming up to the kiosk to have a look at the photo for themselves. We were wettin' ourselves. Craigey eventually got his passport back and, after some pisstaking, we left the arrivals area and got on the tour operators bus to take us to Benidorm. Of course the whole of the bus knew about the passport incident and it was just a matter of time before the whole of Benidorm did too!

On his return, Derek applied for a new passport!!!

12

SHEIKH SHEPHERD

I was absolutely amazed when, in 1998 Freddie Shepherd Jnr, the chairman of Newcastle United, was conned by the fake Sheikh Mazher Mahmood in a sting operation that was to become known as Toon Gate. Why was I so surprised? Well his father Freddie Shepherd Snr. had a habit of dressing up like a Sheikh!

My father was a great friend of Freddie Shepherd Snr. and his brother John, the owners of WF and JR Shepherd, one of the biggest scrap dealers in the North East of England. As a kid, I used to travel on the number 4 Cowgate Circle bus with John Shepherd to watch the Toon play. When I signed for Newcastle it had a lot to do with John and Freddie's powers of persuasion.

As soon as we beat Tottenham Hotspur in the semi final of the League Cup, Freddie Snr. rang me and asked if I could get him some cup final tickets. He said he would take as many as I could get my hands on, pay top whack for them and that there was no risk of me or any of the other players getting into trouble (as the tickets we got were not meant to be sold on) because he would be giving them away to his business associates. Now I know it was wrong to sell tickets to a third party, but the salaries we got in those days were crap (for reasons I have explained in another story) and if you played for Newcastle in the 70's and 80's, you didn't get to a cup final very often, so we felt justified in making a few bob.

I canvassed the other players, explained who the tickets were for and assured them that they would simply be given away to Freddie's business associates. Some of the players agreed to sell to him and some decided to sell to a well known ticket tout in Gateshead. I rang Freddie to give him the good news and I said I would deliver the tickets in a few days. Freddy said no, he wanted to give the money to the players personally and that he'd give them a bit extra for the privilege of doing so. When I explained this to the lads they were initially a bit suspicious. They were afraid they were being set up (it had happened before) and, bear in mind, they had no idea who Freddie Shepherd was. I once again assured them that there was no chance of that (touch wood); Freddie was a huge Newcastle fan and that was why he was prepared to pay above the going rate for the tickets, just to meet the players. The lads were finally convinced and it was arranged that we would meet Freddie at the scrap yard in Byker after training on Friday.

We finished training at around 1pm, got dressed and jumped into our cars and drove to his yard that was situated on Stepney Bank. We climbed the stairs to his office where we were met by his secretary who ushered us into a meeting room. "Freddie will be a couple of minutes" she said, and went to get us some teas and coffees. After a rather tense ten minutes during which the lads kept asking me if everything was ok, i.e. was the room bugged, or had he changed his mind, Freddie entered the room dressed as an Arab Sheikh with both hands holding wads of cash. They looked at Freddie and then at me in total disbelief. "What's the matter" asked Freddie, "Have you never seen money before?" The lads burst out laughing, the tickets and the money changed hands and we proceeded to have a good natter before we left to spend our ill gotten gains in the Pilgrim's Club. Freddie Senior would have turned in his grave knowing his son had been taken in by a fake Sheikh!!!

THE SHEIKH OF BYKER!

13

SIX FOOT TWO, EYES OF BLUE, BIG JIM HOLTON'S GONNA KICK THE SHIT OUT OF YOU!

Gordon Lee, for all his shortcomings, was a tremendous motivator. We were all in the dressing room, an hour before a Tyne/Wear Derby was due to kick off at three o'clock with us at home. Lee pulled me to one side in order to impart some of his football wisdom.

"Jim Holton is playing centre half for them today Paul" he enthused; "You know what he's like…..put yourself about a bit if you know what I mean, I guarantee he'll get himself sent off" …Thanks boss I thought; remembering the chant "Six foot two, eyes of blue, Big Jim Holton's gonna' kick the shit out of you!" Anyways, St. James' Park was packed as usual. There was five minutes left in the first half, I had scored and we were winning 1-0 when our goalkeeper Mick Mahoney booted the ball high downfield. Jim Holton and I rose to head the ball midway in the Sunderland half and I "accidently" smashed him in the mouth with my elbow. He collapsed to the ground; there were teeth and claret all over the St. James' Park turf. If it had happened nowadays with slow motion action replays, I'd have done time! He was stretchered off just before the half time whistle blew and we made our way back to the dressing room. Once inside, Lee put his arm around me, "Great goal Paul and what a great result with Holton; now we've got rid of him go out and get another one" I felt ten feet tall; I'd scored against the Mackems and got rid of Jim Holton! The bell rang in the dressing room to summon the teams onto the pitch for the second half. We took to the pitch first in an atmosphere that only a Tyne/Wear Derby can generate; then the Mackems emerged from the tunnel, one by one and shit, there he was, the third on the pitch…fuckin' Jim Holton!!! I nearly crapped meself!

The second half saw me playing one touch football like never before. I played the second half like my life depended on it…and it probably did! The newspapers the following day commented on our change of tactics in the second half…… "Newcastle, with Cannell playing wide on the right wing….." Do you blame me?

IN THE PICTURE JUST like seven days ago, Newcastle beat Sunderland 2-0 at St James's Park in this December 1976 derby clash. Paul Cannell, seen firing in a header, scored one goal and Alan Kennedy the other. Also pictured are United's Alan Gowling and Wear men Jim Holton, Dick Malone and keeper Barry Siddall.

THIS PICTURE SEZ IT ALL. THERE WASN'T A PHOTOGRAPHER AT ST JAMES' PARK THAT DAY THAT COULD HAVE GOT ME AND JIM HOLTON IN THE SAME FRAME IN THE SECOND HALF WITHOUT A FUCK OFF WIDE ANGLED LENS!

14

MALTA SUNSHINE HOLIDAYS

George Haughton was a typical used car salesman... flash, cash and dodgy! He had set up a new travel company situated on New Bridge Street, Newcastle called Malta Sunshine Holidays, flying punters from Newcastle to Malta direct using Air Malta, the islands national carrier. In order to promote this new venture, he had organised the Newcastle United team to play a game against a Maltese one (Floriana, I believe). The players weren't too keen on this as it was the end of a long season and we basically wanted to go home and relax (get pissed) for a couple of months. We agreed to the trip when we were told we would be staying at the Grand Hotel Verdalla in Rabat, a fantastic five star hotel with all expenses covered. The game, we were told, would be a simple kick around with no pressure, all we had to do was relax and enjoy ourselves in the sunshine for a week.

We arrived in Malta to a fantastic welcome; the PR people for Malta Sunshine Holidays had done their stuff. When we arrived at the hotel it got even better, a chamber orchestra was playing in the huge marbled hotel lobby as we checked in and the champagne flowed. The rooms were twins i.e. two single beds; except for one which was a single. All of the players insisted I got the single room (usually they fought not to share a room!) due to the fact that I snored like a pig. In fact, Mick Mahoney said that last time he shared a room with me it was like the exorcist, the drawers were moving in and out and the curtains were blowing in time to my snoring.

It was four days until the game; the management were true to their word, no training, unlimited alcohol and plenty of trips to the red light district of Gzira. The night before the game was a really heavy night, drinks by the pool, into the bar then down to the night clubs of Paceville and Sliema. Not all the players participated; there were half a dozen sensible ones that stayed at the hotel. I won't embarrass them by naming them. But I, along with Mick Mahoney, Alan Kennedy and Tommy Cassidy all indulged in the delights of Malta's night life. We arrived back at the hotel just in time for breakfast with the management, members of the Maltese football club and of course the press (mind you, a lot of the press had been out with us!). We were told to be in the hotel lobby after lunch to take the team bus to the Maltese stadium in Gzira.

FUCKIN' HELL IT'S PAUL CANNELL

**WILLIE McFAUL, ALAN KENNEDY, ME AND HALF OF STEWY BARRACLOUGH
GETTING READY FOR THE MATCH. YOU COULDN'T SEE FOR THE FUCKIN'
SUN!**

It was only a fifteen minute ride (everything is only a fifteen minute ride
as you will know if you have ever been to Malta) to the stadium. I'd never
noticed before that the Maltese drove on both sides of the road and that you could
go either way round a roundabout or even over it! On arrival at the stadium we
were welcomed by a large crowd that, as we were leaving the bus, waved wads of
bank notes in our faces trying to bribe us into losing the game. If they had known
how we felt, they could have saved their energy!

The temperature was over one hundred degrees Fahrenheit (I don't think
Celsius had been invented back then) and on entering the stadium we were totally
taken aback. The pitch was 100% white dust, not a blade of grass in sight. It was
so white that the goal posts were painted in black and white bands, not because it
was Newcastle's colours but to enable the players to see the goals against the

white glare of the pitch. We didn't bother to warm up, we just sat in the dressing room (if you could call it a dressing room, it was more like something the French Foreign Legion would hold their prisoners in!) sweating and being sick! Then we realised we had an even bigger problem, the only boots we had brought with us were studs, absolutely useless on this cement like surface.

THE GZIRA PITCH, IT WAS LIKE PLAYING ON A CAR PARK WHILST WEARING STUDS AND VOMITING. IT'S JUST AS WELL THE GOAL POSTS WERE PAINTED BLACK AND WHITE SO WE DIDN'T BUMP INTO THEM COS' WE COULD SEE FUCK ALL!

All of a sudden the manager, Gordon Lee, stood up to deliver a team talk. Gone were the phrases "it's just a kick about" "just enjoy it" and "the score means nowt" and in came the phrases "I want 100%" "We've got our reputation to think about" and "I want ninety minutes of real hard graft".

By the time we left the dressing room, half the players were seriously dehydrated and were still being sick; then we had to go onto the pitch - which was like walking on red hot coals. Thankfully our studs kept us about three quarters of an inch above the concrete hard surface that was proverbially hot enough to fry an egg on! The stadium was packed, we never realised just how many Geordies holidayed in Malta. We tried our best but to no avail.

34

FUCKIN' HELL IT'S PAUL CANNELL

Mick Mahoney had to leave the goal several times to go and relieve himself from both ends, I think that Alan Kennedy and I were sick on each other at a corner kick and, although the dressing room stunk like a sewer, they had to drag us out of it for the second half with threats of law suits and fines. I can't even remember the final score (now or at the end of the game) however someone told me back at the hotel that he thought we had lost 1-0. There may have been some truth in this as, at the start of pre season training, a Maltese player joined us on trial. His name was Ray Xureb and we became good friends; we didn't sign him, but I did visit him several times in Malta in the following years and he'd often take great delight in reminding me that he had scored against us.

We spent our last couple of days in Malta hanging out with the supporters who'd travelled over to watch the game as well as the Maltese Newcastle United supporters club. They forgave us for our shambolic performance but reminded us of the saying 'There is no such thing as an easy football match"
Party-wise, it turned out to be a great trip and I fell in love with Malta and the 'Maltesers'. I have visited there several times since, but never to play football...

P.S. George Houghton and Malta Sunshine Holidays were very happy with the trip and went on to sell thousands of holidays to Malta over many years. George went on to become chairman of Darlington Football Club I do believe.

15

THE WITCH QUEEN OF CRAWCROOK

Billy the Pie and I (like it?) were in the La Dolce Vita nightclub and sitting opposite us were two fit lasses. "I don't like yours" I said to 'the pie' as I got up to ask them if they fancied a dance, but Billy got up anyway as he was canny like that. We had a couple of dances then sat down and started talking. It transpired that they worked in the Swallow hotel in the centre of Newcastle as chambermaids; the same hotel that Gordon Lee and Richard Dinnis were staying in while they were waiting to move into permanent accommodation. I'd only been getting the occasional game in the first team and Stephanie (the good looking one I was with) suggested she should have a word with them to get me more games. I took it as a bit of a laugh; I mean what could she do? Anyway, as the night drew to a close, Stephanie and I left Billy with her mate and we drove to the Swallow hotel where she said she was staying that night, as she had an early start in the morning.

I continued seeing her for the next few weeks (even though I was still engaged to my long time girlfriend Julie) always meeting her, never picking her up from home. She was a strange lass, tall, beautiful, intelligent; but a bit strange. I couldn't quite put my finger on it (no, I did put me finger on that) All the lads had seen me with her and thought she was gorgeous..... but a bit strange. Time passed and I was seeing her more and more often and I was getting more and more games for the first team. Stephanie told me that she thought it odd that quite often, only one bed had been slept in by Gordon Lee and Richard Dinnis when they both had separate but adjoining rooms in the hotel; and she should know, she did their rooms! Then, one Monday, as we were getting changed for training, Tommy Craig came up to me and asked if I had read the Sunday Sun yesterday. I said I hadn't but asked why, was there something in it about Saturday's game?. No he replied it's your lass, her with the long black hair; she's a witch!

I couldn't wait to get a hold of the paper. When I did, there it was in black and white 'HEADLESS CHICKENS FOUND IN CRAWCROOK.' Seemingly a woman had been held for questioning after being found at the site of a well

36

known witches' coven, in Crawcrook along with several headless chickens (so that's where the phrase comes from). Right next to the story was a picture of wor' lass! I went back home after training to me mam and dad's house and just as I got in, the phone rang, it was Stephanie. Had anyone seen the paper she asked, Yes, I replied the whole of the Newcastle team as well as the entire circulation of the fuckin' Sunday Sun! She apologised for not telling me about her hobby and she hoped it wouldn't spoil our relationship. I assured her it would not as, to tell you the truth; I found it a bit of a turn on. However things started getting a bit weirder. When I used to get home on a Friday lunchtime after training, I would find little cloth bags full of soil or dressed clothes pegs or little handmade dolls pushed through the letterbox; then I would get a phone call asking if we could do all sorts of things that I would find hard to do on a weekday, never mind on the day before a match! I started making excuses not to see her; to try to distance the relationship but she would just turn up or stuff something else through the fuckin' door.

Things eventually settled down when she took over the Ryton Country Club and I fucked off to America. Looking back though, she was gorgeous, she was definitely interesting and I did start to play regularly for the first team. Oh, and the rumour about Gordon Lee and Richard Dinnis….. Well late one night/ early morning, they had to get their car towed off Tynemouth Beach after getting stuck in the sand whilst watching the sunrise together!!

THIS ISN'T STEPHANIE, BUT SHE WAS A CANNY LOOKING WITCH!

16

SUPERMAC

Mal was me best mate at Newcastle. I was kind of his understudy but we got on really well. People thought he was a brash, big headed, cocky cockney but nothing could have been further from the truth. He was breath taking on the football pitch; can you imagine what he would be worth in today's transfer market, he'd be worth more than our national debt. I'll always remember him on the TV series Superstars when, with no starting blocks and wearing a pair of school plimsolls, he ran the 100 yards in an Olympic qualifying time!

He never had the best of luck with his cars. He once had a TVR sports car and the gearbox fell out on the Great North Road on the way to training causing traffic chaos. He also had a Ferrari that he had to drive in his slippers because he had gout (probably from the port we used to drink at the Astor Club after training!) and the vibration coming through the cars foot controls was knackin' him.

Mal, I love him; I was really happy when he married another good friend of mine, Carole Johnson, the ex wife of AC/DC's Brian Johnson, another Geordie legend. Malcolm's favourite party trick was hypnosis with a difference. He would get a candle and an empty bottle of wine, light the candle and then hold the bottle horizontally at eye level with the lit candle behind the base of the bottle. He would then ask his victim to concentrate on the candle whilst stroking their face gently. What his victim didn't know was that he'd scraped soot from the base of the bottle (caused by the burning candle) onto his finger and was painting it on their face. Eventually he would stop, saying that he was giving up because the subject just could not be hypnotised. The hapless victim would then wander around with a blackened face, sometimes for ages, before someone gave the game away. Normally it would result in good laugh but he once tried it in the Pilgrim's Club, a rough all day drinking den in Jesmond, Newcastle. The girl who he 'hypnotised' had been wandering around the club for ages in total ignorance. Unfortunately her boyfriend arrived who happened to be one of Newcastle's hard men and he did not see the funny side of it. We made our excuses and legged it!

THIS WAS A FUCKIN' BACK PASS!!!

17

'JINKY' JIMMY SMITH

Jimmy Smith was my idol as a kid. I've still got his autograph even though I've given the likes of Richard Nixon's and Pele's away! I'd had a season ticket for the Toon long before I signed for them and I loved watching 'Jinky', he was so laid back and had sublime skills. The way he could drag the ball back with the outside of his foot and nutmeg a player who was coming in to flatten him was, as they would say now, 'awesome'!

ME, SOMEBODY ELSE AND 'JINKY' HAD "GONE TO THE DOGS"

When I signed for the Toon I discovered that Jimmy's priorities were gambling, women, drinking Bacardi and Cokes and the nightclubs... but that didn't stop thirty thousand Newcastle fans turning up for a reserve match, simply cos' Jinky was playing I'll never ever forget the game against Wolverhampton Wanderers when Jimmy was being marked by Mike Bailey who, at the time, was an England international. Jinky nutmegged him time and time again. The more he tried to clatter Jinky, the more he got nutmegged; it was like watching the matador against the bull. Bailey was quoted in the newspapers the next day saying he'd never had such a showing up on a football pitch! Jinky was often, especially by the Chronicle's John Gibson, called an 'enigma'.....but he was a fuckin' entertainin' enigma!

'JINKY' JIMMY SMITH

18

A BLAST FROM THE PAST...

FRANK CLARK, ME, SUPERMAC AND ALAN KENNEDY AT THE RECORDING STUDIO.
NOTE: NOT A MICROPHONE IN SIGHT!

When I read in the Evening Chronicle that a reader had unearthed a record by the Newcastle United cup squad that had been lost for over thirty years I was more than a little surprised! I've got a box full here! However it did bring back some good memories.

We'd been contacted by the Evening Chronicle to see if we'd be interested in recording a song with a bloke called Bobby Webber, a song which had, I believe, been written by Mike Mason of Mike Mason and the Little People; a band well known on the North East social club circuit. Bobby was well known to the Newcastle players as he had been a great supporter of both Frank Clark's and David Craig's testimonials. We recorded the song at the Impulse recording studios in Newcastle that I was told had something to do with the band Lindisfarne. Some of the records were given away by the Chronicle; the remainder were released on the Airborne record label and were sold in record shops in the Newcastle area.

During the recording I had a natter with Bobby in which I agreed to go round the social clubs in the area with him, promoting and selling the single. I didn't take much persuading; after all, I did like a pint.

Once we embarked on our 'tour' I met some of Bobbie's mates; Billy Robinson, Paddy Leonard, Derek Lang, The Yank (John Ekstridge) and Nodge to name but a few; all of whom could be described as 'loveable rogues.' We spent several weeks ' touring' during which time I got to know Bobbie's stage act off by heart. We sold a load of records, mostly down to Billie's powers of persuasion and, I like to think, we all became good friends. Billie used to run the door at a nightclub in Gateshead called Wheelers; it was a bit rough but good fun. When I used to come home during the off season in America, I used to catch up with them there. One particular visit I made to the club stands out. I had read in the local paper that a man had died after falling down the stairs in Wheelers. When I got to the club, I asked Billie about the incident and he explained to me that the bloke was ok the first time he 'fell down the stairs'......I think he was kiddin'!!!!!

19

GRAB A GRANNY NIGHT

To say that footballers in the seventies and the eighties didn't have the same lifestyle as the pampered football millionaires of today, is a gross understatement! The highlight of our week was a Monday night at the Forest Hall Social club for the 'grab a granny' night. Actually that title is not strictly true as there were some very fit young bits of stuff got in there. It was always packed to the rafters, so much so, that you had to queue up to get a ticket prior to the doors opening at 7.30pm. The fact that you were a Newcastle United player made no difference whatsoever to the committee at Forest Hall; you still had to have a ticket. Now, because I lived the closest to the club, I had the job of obtaining tickets for the likes of Malcolm McDonald, Alan Kennedy, Mick Mahoney and 'Jinky' Jimmy Smith to name but a few. I had to be in the queue at 6.30pm, which meant I missed my favourite TV show at the time, Star Trek (sad, I know).

FOREST HALL SOCIAL CLUB, HARDLY STUDIO 54!
TRY GETTIN' SOME FUCKER TO SIGN YOU IN, IN THOSE DAYS, EVEN IF YOU DID PLAY FOR THE TOON!

FUCKIN' HELL IT'S PAUL CANNELL

The evening was always entertaining. The DJ was also the concert chairman and he was in his eighties, stone deaf and he could never accurately put the needle on the start of the vinyl records due to his rapidly failing sight. And you should have seen him doin' the bingo!

Fortunately, as it was on a Monday, it was usually ok for us to get pissed….. Which you had to be to dance the Bradford Barn! If you hadn't pulled by closing time you headed down to Whitley Bay and onto the Sands club where, if you had most of your original limbs, you were guaranteed to pull! Aye, footballers of today don't know what they missed!!!!!

20

THE PLAYERS' STRIKE

With the departure of Gordon Lee to Everton, the management situation at Newcastle United needed to be sorted and many names were being bandied about. The 'committee' in the dressing room however, had their own agenda; they wanted Lee's right hand man Richard Dinnis to take over. The 'committee' consisted of Geoff Nulty, Tommy Craig, Alan Gowling and Mickey Burns, all of whom (as did most of the players) thought very highly of Dinnis.

We held a players meeting at which it was decided that the players would walk out on strike if Dinnis was not given the job. In order to announce this to the world, it was decided that we would give a press conference, however none of the 'committee' would participate. The job was given to the local lads, Alan Kennedy, Irving Nattrass and me. A clever move as the committee was still seen to be implicated in the departure of Toon legends Malcolm McDonald and Terry Hibbitt.

At the time, the bookies had Dinnis as an outsider for the job at odds of around 25-1. When the idea of a players strike was suggested, one of the younger players dashed down to Ladbrokes and, still in his training gear, put a bet of £20 on him. This caused his price to fall to around 5-1 making Dinnis one of the favourites and upsetting many of the senior players who had seen a chance of making some easy money.

The directors eventually caved in and Richard Dinnis was given the managerial role. The remainder of the season went well and we eventually finished either fourth or fifth top, I can't remember which exactly, of the First Division and qualified, for the first time in many years, for Europe.

Richard was a good bloke however he was always perceived to be too close to the players... and the directors didn't like that! He also made some questionable decisions, such as the location of our first pre-season training under him. He decided to take the first team squad to Zandvoort, a seaside resort, a few kilometres from Amsterdam. This was supposed to be a week of intense stamina building; it turned out to be a week of intense drinking and debauchery that both required a great degree of stamina! Even the newspaper reporters, who accompanied us on the trip, struggled to keep up (and jeez could they party). I'll never forget Mick Mahoney, our first team goalkeeper, staggering, aimlessly, along the beach in his club suit, wearing a pair of Cuban heels, swigging a bottle of Amstel at 3 o'clock in the afternoon!

The season started and it was no surprise that, after our pre-season, things didn't go too well in the league; but we were still in Europe, so Richard's job was safe for the time being. After getting past Bohemians we were drawn against the Corsican club Bastia, whose star player was the Dutch legend Johnny Rep. We did our research on Bastia and one of the things we discovered was quite disconcerting.

In a previous game, one of Bastia's opponents had had a goal disallowed because, as the ball was about to cross the goal line, a fan (I presume a Bastia fan) had shot the ball. Even though it finished up in the back of the net, the referee had to disallow the goal because the ball was 'bust' (not the correct pressure or circumference) when it had crossed the line. So we should have been prepared for anything on our trip to Corsica.

IRVING NATRASS, PETER KELLY, TOMMY CASSIDY, SOME FRENCH TWAT, ME, STEVEY HARDWICK AND BARRA, BEING NICE TO THE FROGGIES IN CASE WE GOT SHOT!

FUCKIN' HELL IT'S PAUL CANNELL

We arrived on the island a couple of days before the first leg and were afforded, what we were led to believe, was typical Corsican hospitality. We trained in the afternoon on their pitch which was small, as was their stadium; it only held around 10,000 spectators at the most. We returned to the hotel, had our evening meal and were 'put to bed' around 11pm. That's when a disco started, deafening music that made it almost impossible to sleep. The same thing happened again the following night so, on the day before the match, the players were feeling tired to say the least. However, our Corsican hosts apologized and said they had arranged a sightseeing tour for us and the coach would pick us up at teatime.

We boarded the bus looking forward to a nice relaxing tour of the island, what we got was a three hour white knuckle ride over mountainous terrain with a formula one bus driver who was high on LSD! There was more fuckin' prayin' done on that bus than in the whole of the fuckin' Vatican City. When we eventually made it back to the team hotel we were exhausted and shaking like leaves. So much for Corsican Hospitality...

The actual match went off quite canny. Although we lost 2-1 we played well, I scored a goal (from all of a yard out) and we kept the famed Johnny Rep in check. We felt quite confident, on the way home, that we could overturn the one goal deficit. Tommy Craig was quoted as saying "Who is this Johnny Rep that we have heard so much about?"

The second leg came around and in front of a packed St James' Park we got stuffed 3-1. Tommy Craig was forced to eat his words when Johnny Rep scored a wonder goal; I remember being nutmegged by him some 30 yards out, turning around and seeing the ball in the roof of our net in the blink of an eye. Europe was gone and Richard Dinnis was soon to follow.

21

GETTIN' HER LOG OVER

It was September 14th 1977; we were in Dublin playing Bohemians in the UEFA cup after qualifying in fourth place (I remembered) in the first division. It was at the height of the troubles in Ireland and everyone was a little nervous as there had been threats made against all English teams visiting the Emerald Isle.

Football wise, the game had been pretty uneventful; however, as we left the pitch at half time, we were bombarded with bricks, bottles and cans but fortunately no incendiary devices resulting in the second half being delayed until the police had restored order. The game restarted and continued with no more incidents; we were more than happy to leave the pitch with a goal less draw, and no casualties.

Back at the Burlington Hotel in the fashionable area of the capital, the drinks were flowing as we celebrated not getting beaten and not getting killed! The Irish F.A. had organised 'a bit of a do' to commemorate the game. There was a band playing in the ballroom and the lads were doing what they do normally when they are pissed and away from home....they were looking for women.

There were four of us at our table, myself, Tommy Cassidy, Alan Kennedy and Mick Mahoney if I remember correctly. "Look at her" whispered Alan to me, "she's fucking gorgeous". I looked at who he was pointing out and agreed. "She looks like she's getting a lot of attention, she must be someone special" I said. Like real adults we dared each other who would have the nerve to ask her up to dance (well it's better than seeing who can pull the ugliest bird, aye, you've all done that haven't you!). Never dare a drunken fool. Up I got and well, I didn't exactly saunter over to her table, I stumbled over cos' I was pissed and limping as I had torn a hamstring muscle during the game.

"Hi'ya pet, would you like a dance?" I asked her... as I looked back at our table and saw them all pissing themselves laughing. "Are you sure you can manage it with your bad leg?" replied the goddess in a silky Irish accent. "Why aye pet, no problem. Were you at the match tonight?" I asked "Yes" she replied. "I'm a sports presenter for Television RTE." "I'm in here" I thought as I held out my hand to lead her to the dance floor. As soon as she stood up and started walking, my heart sank. I could tell by the way she hobbled along that she had a

49

major movement malfunction! Still, I had to go through with it as the lads were all watching, I was drunk and she was still fuckin' gorgeous. The first dance was a dream, a nice slow smoochie number, no problems, a little ear whispering, a little bit of begging and a few white lies, such as, "Eee pet, a didn't realise you had a wooden leg!" However, the next number the band played was only a bloody jive wasn't it...? Now, I'm not the best dancer in the world, especially with a girl who I was now convinced had a wooden leg. After the first few twirls, I grabbed her tightly and started smooching again; I was terrified in case her leg became unscrewed! "Don't worry" she whispered in my ear, "it's only the Twist that gives me problems".

As the night passed and the Guinness flowed, I forgot about the absence of a leg and concentrated on the attributes that were there. I sensed that the time had come for me to ask her if she fancied staying the night, so I did. "No" she replied. "I've got to get home, I only live up the road, would you like to come back to mine?" Daft question, of course I would. We left the Burlington and limped in unison up the road to her home, a beautiful mews style house, a few minutes limp from the hotel.

AS THEIR ADVERTS SAY "IF WALLS COULD SPEAK, THE BURLINGTON HOTEL DUBLIN WOULD TELL A TALE OR TWO"

FUCKIN' HELL IT'S PAUL CANNELL

To be perfectly honest, I was that pissed I can't even remember what happened after that. She may have taken advantage of me or she may not. However I woke up in bed next to her, starker's and badly hung over, trying to get my bearings. After a few minutes, it all started coming back to me. I looked over at the clock, it was 7am. I had to get back to the hotel as we were leaving at 7.30am.for the airport. Rather than waking her, I decided to be a gentleman and simply sneak out; however it was still quite dark and the curtains were still closed.

I slid silently out of the bed, being careful not to let the wooden flooring squeak. Shirt on, underpants on, socks on, club suit jacket on, club suit trousers..., club suit trousers...where the fuck are they. Stumbling around in the dark, trying to be quiet so she didn't wake up, I eventually found what I thought were my trousers. Try as I might, I just couldn't get them on properly in the dark. She suddenly stirred and I thought she might be waking up. "I've got to get out" I thought as I sneaked down the stairs only stopping briefly to put my shoes on. Out the door and onto the high street… only to find that I was wearing her luminous, lime green trousers which were excruciatingly tight in all the wrong places!

The looks I got as I walked back to the hotel, the grey club suit jacket teamed with a pair of embarrassingly ill fitting shiny lime green women's flared pants; I got wolf whistles, cars honking their horns at me and then the lads really took the piss when I got back to the hotel! It was night to remember!

22

MAGIC MAGPIE MOMENTS

My time at my home town club Newcastle enabled me to play with some terrific players and spend real quality time with some huge characters.

When I first signed for the Toon I was 'educated' by some of the most dedicated professionals in the game. Fullbacks Frank Clark and David Craig, centre half Bobby Moncur and goalkeeper Willie McFaul were always willing to give advice and, even though they were established internationals, were never 'above' the younger players. They were never really recognised as ultra skilful players but their work ethic was second to none. I'll never forget the night Clarky scored his first goal for Newcastle after umpteen seasons. You'd think, by the reaction of the fans, we'd won the cup!

When it came to pure skill, two players stand out a mile. 'Jinky' Jimmy Smith and Tony Green. Both players, sadly, had their careers cut short by injuries but the time they did spend on the pitch at St James' Park was, to me, truly magical.

When it came to strikers, I had the honour to play with some of the best. John Tudor, a lovely bloke and one of the best headers of the ball in the business and Mickey Burns, a quick very clever player and a very wise individual. Then there was Alan Gowling, slightly ungainly in a Peter Crouch sort of way but a smashing team player and goal scorer, and then there was Supermac, Malcolm McDonald. In my opinion, at the height of his career, he was the best, most exciting goal scorer in the world. He was good in the air, fast as fuck and as strong as a horse. It's hard to believe that he started out as a fullback!

Apart from Willie McFaul, who was nearing the end of his career, the best goalkeeper I played with was Mick Mahoney (Super Goalie) a larger than life character who hailed from the Wurzel part of the country, around Bristol. After a Saturday match he would often drive back home and return on the Monday, laden with flagons of genuine scrumpy that was pure rocket fuel. I actually played against Mick in America, during the indoor soccer season, where I believe he has since made his home.

Some of the younger players I grew up with included Eric Steele, a goalkeeper who had a longer career than most; after leaving Newcastle he played for several clubs, and is, at the time I'm writing this, the current Manchester United goalkeeping coach.

Ray 'Rocky' Hudson was a great prospect but never quite made it at Newcastle. He, like meself, ended up playing in America where he eventually became the manager of DC United. He lost that job after trying to sign Paul Gascoigne (enough said!). Alan Kennedy (or Budgie to his mates) and I grew up in the Newcastle reserve team. He was a tenacious full back, who ended up winning European cup medals for Liverpool.

Stewart Barrowclough and Irving Nattrass were great friends with each other (in fact at one time I believe they shared the same girlfriend). The former was an excellent, skilful winger, the latter, an elegant full back or half back. What they had in common was they both loved The Dolce nightclub.

People often ask me what are the lasting memories that I have from playing for the Toon and what were the best goals that I scored. When it comes to lasting memories it has to be our away supporters. It didn't matter if it was Walsall in the FA Cup, Bastia in the UEFA Cup or Sunderland in a Tyne/Wear derby; they were always there in their thousands. So consistent was the support that the players, in those days, actually got to know some of the supporters personally.

My most memorable goals? Well they're all memorable aren't they but I'm most often asked about the goal I scored against Leeds United at Elland Road and whether it was a cross or a shot. I remember receiving the ball just inside the Leeds United half, wide on the right wing. I put my head down and started running like fuck. I was actually waiting to be put into the crowd as the Leeds team was composed of players such as Norman 'Bites Y'er Legs' Hunter, Paul Madeley, Billy Bremner and Johnny Giles to name but a few, all of whom would have no hesitation in taking the man and not the ball! After what seemed like ages, I realised that I still had the ball, I was still upright and I was still running. I thought if I didn't do something soon I'd end up running into the crowd of Newcastle supporters behind the home team's goal. I let fly with my right foot just before I reached the corner flag. I looked up and, I don't know who was more surprised me or David Harvey (the Leeds United goalkeeper) when I saw the ball spinning in the roof of the net. There were thousands of Newcastle supporters behind that goal who all went berserk and, in all the years that have passed, I think I must have met every single one of them and they have all asked me whether or not it was intended as a shot at goal. My answer is that it was most definitely a shot at goal... however, if I'd known where I was, then it would most definitely have been a cross! I also try to remind them that I did score quite a few other goals for the Toon!

23

THE CLASH

I still can't believe that I ended up living and playing football in the United States of America. Although I'd thoroughly enjoyed my loan spell in the US in 1976, Newcastle was still my home.

Back in Newcastle, we'd started the season off under new manager Gordon Lee brilliantly, not playing the most attractive football, but getting the results. However, three quarters of the way through the season, Lee left for Everton and his right hand man Richard Dinnis took over. We ended the season qualifying for Europe which was quite an achievement. However the following season we had a crap start and eventually, after the dreaded vote of confidence, Dinnis was sacked to be replaced by, to me, the most miserable man in the world of football, Bill McGarry.

McGarry should never have been a football manager, his favourite sport was squash. He liked to challenge the players to a game as he was a really good player. I soon realised he and I would never get on when, one afternoon, he asked me "Cannell, do you like squash?" and I replied "yes with a vodka and a lot of ice." Bye, bye, Paul!

In my opinion he quite simply wasn't a nice man; you can come into a new club, assess the situation, and then go about rectifying the problems you have identified without being an obnoxious knob head. I remember two ludicrous rules that he implemented.

The first was a ban on players buying sweets and crisps on away trips, a major coup! When playing away games, most of the travelling was done by coach. Obviously, when going long distances, the coach would have to stop at motorway services to re-fuel. The norm was for the players to dive out, have a piss and buy some magazines, sweets, crisps etc, all a good source of carbohydrates, well aren't they? McGarry totally frowned upon this and banned the players from buying snacks when the bus stopped to re-fuel. But he couldn't stop the players from having a piss now could he? (Although he would if he could). Alan Kennedy, the only player I ever knew who had to leave the pitch during a match to go for a crap, couldn't kick his crisp habit. It meant he had to go to the services toilets and then sneakily buy his bag of Tudors. How pitiful was it to watch a grown man sit in the back seat of a bus and suck crisps in order not to make a giveaway crunching noise.

His other ludicrous rule was aimed at the players who were on the injury list. Since I joined the club, if you were injured, you had your treatment, did any medical/physio exercises that were required and then you were either sent home or made to come back for a second session in the afternoon. For some reason McGarry was obsessed with players faking injury. His new rule was for the injured players to go for a walk along a certain route, after their treatment, to stop them from going home!

What he didn't realise was that his route took the players past the New Kent Hotel in Jesmond where the owner, Alan, would always give us a pint; then past the Lonsdale, the North Terrace and the Black Bull, where, in each of these fine drinking establishments, the bar staff were only too willing to rehydrate the injured Newcastle players!

I had been informed that the Washington Diplomats wanted to sign me on a permanent basis and so I wasn't prepared to put up with any shit from the arrogant McGarry. Don't get me wrong, I always knew I wasn't the greatest footballer in the world but I always gave 100% and I needed to enjoy what I was doing.

At a talk- in at a local social club, someone asked me what I thought about Bill McGarry. My reply was, "If I was standing on the Tyne Bridge, threatening to jump and he came to talk me down, I'd aim for the fuckin' pavement below, not the water!" Enough said. I returned to Washington D.C. soon afterwards.

MANAGER BILL McGARRY. THE MOST MISERABLE, ARROGANT BLOKE I'VE EVER MET. LOOKS LIKE HE HAD BOTOX!!!

FUCKIN' HELL IT'S PAUL CANNELL
HAVIN' A CRAP!

FUCK KNOWS WHY GRAHAM OATES TOOK THIS PICTURE OF ME DURING PRE SEASON TRAINING IN ZANDVOORT BUT HE DID!

STAR SPANGLED SOCCER

MY PART IN ITS' DOWNFALL

24

LEAVIN' ON A JET PLANE

How on earth did a Toon loving Geordie lad who wouldn't move to Leeds United, Blackburn Rovers or Luton Town in order to further his career, end up playing in America? It was all John Bird's fault.

Birdie and I were playing for the reserves against Manchester United at Old Trafford one Saturday afternoon. I didn't realise it but Dennis Viollet (an Old Trafford legend and survivor of the Munich air disaster), was in the crowd running his eyes over John. Dennis was the manager of the Washington Diplomats, a fairly new franchise that had just moved from the American Soccer League to the newly formed North American Soccer League. I must have had a good game because when the final whistle blew, Birdie pulled me to one side and told me that Dennis had had a word with him and asked if he thought I'd be interested in going over to play for the Diplomats on loan that summer.

It didn't take long, after speaking to Dennis, to make my mind up. He was a wonderful man with a vast knowledge of the game and he had a great vision for football in America. "Enjoy yourself for three months, play against Pele'and pull the birds." It sounded pretty good to me!

So, from being the stay at home Geordie kid, I was suddenly booked on a flight to Washington DC. I have to thank Gordon Lee, the new Toon manager, because it was him who encouraged me all the way. "Enjoy yourself and come back a better player" were his parting words at the end of the season.

It didn't take me long to realise that football in the U.S. was a bit different to the English first division. I landed at Dulles airport in Virginia and was picked up by the Diplomats trainer, Tim; the rest of the team were in Dallas for a game the following night. I was to stay with Tim that night, then he would take me the following day to National Airport for a flight to Dallas to meet up with the rest of the Dips (as they were nicknamed) and I was to play my first game against the Dallas Tornadoes.

When we arrived at his house I was immediately offered a beer. In England, drinking the day before a match was severely frowned upon so, quite honestly, I wasn't used to it. As time went by, more and more people arrived, more beer was supped and then 'cigarettes' started getting passed around. Now I know this might sound naive, but I thought that these people looked quite well off and I wondered why they were sharing cigarettes. I wasn't, and I had never been a smoker but, when I was offered a drag, I felt it might be impolite to refuse. The cigarettes continued to circulate around what was now a bit of a party with music blaring, people disappearing to adjoining rooms and me having what I was later to be informed was my first 'whitey'. The symptoms of my first whitey were simple...it took me over an hour to get myself into a toilet and organise having a piss! A short while later there was a sudden crashing noise as the front door was caved in followed by a shitload of police. I however, was totally cabbaged. I had to fumble through my suitcases to find my passport in order to convince them I was not a drug smokin' illegal immigrant, that I had a current visa, that I was the newest member of the Washington Diplomats soccer team and that I had nothing to do with the noise, the car crash outside (which I only found out about later) or the drugs that the neighbours had complained about. Welcome to the USA.

I woke in the morning, sitting on what was now a mate of mine, yes, the toilet, wondering where the hell I was. After several minutes, Tim the trainer found me and apologized profusely for the party ending early and told me to get ready as I had a plane to catch.

1976 DIPLOMATS

Standing Left to Right: Dennis Viollet (Coach/Manager), Paul Cannell, Don Reiter, Roy Ellam, Alain Maca, Eric Martin, John Grasser, Gary Darrell, Stojan Trickovic, Tom McConville (Captain), Trevor Thompson.
Kneeling Left to Right: Alan Spavin (Assistant Coach), Tony Macken, Leroy DeLeon, Roger Minton, Roy Willner, Mark Lowenstein, Gerry Ingram, John Kerr.

THE 1976 WASHINGTON DIPLOMATS LOOKED A MOTLEY CREW... AND WE WERE!

FUCKIN' HELL IT'S PAUL CANNELL

I couldn't believe that I was on my way to play my first match in America after having my first experience of marijuana, downing gallons of Bud and almost being arrested. Needless to say, I slept on the flight. After landing in Dallas Fort Worth, I was picked up by Dennis Viollet who simply looked at me and said "I hope your flight was ok, we kick off in two hours." We made our way to the Tornadoes stadium where I was hurriedly introduced to my new team mates and given the number nine shirt with my name on the back. Talk about being thrown in at the deep end...

We left the dressing room and I can honestly say that, with the effects of the previous night still heavily lingering over me, the seven hour time difference as well as jet lag, I was not in the best frame of mind to make my debut appearance for the Dips. Things got worse. The pitch was painted red white and blue, not a patch of green anywhere. Our captain Alan Spavin won the toss and, for a reason I was to find out soon, he decided to kick off. Now normally, if you win the toss, you decide in which direction you want to play, however this game was being kicked off by an elephant, yes you heard right, a fuckin' elephant!. So the protocol was, you kept possession of the ball until the elephant left the pitch; only then did the game officially start.

Welcome to Star Spangled Soccer. I loved it!!!

25

CAFÉ DE PARIS

The Café de Paris was on M Street in Georgetown and it was the place where soccer fans and players hung out; not because of the great food but because Michel, the restaurant's owner, had ran a soccer team for years, long before soccer had become fashionable in the States.

One evening, there were a few of us sitting at the bar, just chatting amongst ourselves about recent games and recent women. At the same time, this couple were having a romantic dinner, whispering sweet nothings, and all that, in each other's ear. They were seated facing each other, with the woman's back to the far wall. Above her head was a loudspeaker playing that fuckin' awful French restaurant background music. For some reason, our conversation turned to this couple. We were just remarking on how much in love they appeared and how gorgeous she looked when the bracket holding the loudspeaker snapped and, in what seemed like slow motion, the speaker fell onto the woman's head pushing her face into her soup.

Michel's jaw dropped as he muttered words such as "Lawyers, law suits, compensation......" There was a stony silence throughout the restaurant as the woman slowly lifted her face from out of the restaurants famous French onion soup with as much dignity as she could muster. Her partner tried like hell to hold it together but he failed miserably. He burst out laughing, not the wisest thing to do as he ended up wearing not only what was left of her French onion soup but also his own! She stormed out of the restaurant and onto a busy M street, followed sheepishly by him, whilst the rest of the restaurant watched the cabaret totally engrossed.

For the next few months we kept asking Michel if he'd heard from the couple or their lawyers but he said he hadn't. He did add however that they had never been back for a meal either!

26

IF IT MOVES KICK IT, IF IT DOESN'T MOVE, KICK IT TIL IT DOES

"It's a funny old game" is a phrase associated with football the world over and it really summed up my relationship with Scottish defender Jimmy Steele.

Jimmy was an animal of a centre half who played for Southampton in the seventies, and guess who Newcastle were playing in the final of the Texaco Cup.... Yes, Southampton. To reach the final we'd been beaten 2-1 by Sunderland (shit), drawn 2-2 with Carlisle United, and stuffed Middlesbrough 4-0 to win our group (due to bonus points for goals scored). We went on to beat Aberdeen 4-3 on aggregate in the quarter finals, then beat Birmingham City on aggregate in the semi final.

We played the first leg of the final at the Dell in Southampton where we lost 1-0 which was not bad as the Saints had an impressive home record. The second leg was played on a freezing cold Wednesday night. The first leg had been quite rough so Gordon Hill, who was generally regarded (amongst the players at least) to be the best referee in the world, was chosen to officiate the second leg at St James' Park. What made Hill so special to the players was the fact that he spoke the player's language. If you moaned at one of his decisions, he was likely to retort with something like "I'm having a hard time but I'm not having a fuckin' nightmare like you!" He got the players respect.

The game was frantic with knee high tackles, going over the top, elbows and punches... and that was just Jimmy Steele! John Tudor scored during regulation time, which made it 1-1 on aggregate, and so the game went to extra time. After a few minutes of extra time, Steeley upended me for the umpteenth time which resulted in Gordon Hill reaching into his pocket. He pulled out a yellow card but then realised he'd already given him one and quickly changed it for a red one and Steeley had to leave the field of play. The look on Gordon's face was strange, he looked genuinely upset. Not something you would expect from such a highly experienced referee. Anyway the game continued and we took full advantage of our extra player. Alec Bruce scored making it 2-1 and I finished it off which resulted in us winning 3-1 and lifting the Texaco Cup for the second time. The officials went up to collect their mementoes from the Texaco officials with Gordon Hill still looking miserable and subdued (anyone would have thought he had good money on Southampton to win!). Typically, for Newcastle United, we were presented not with winner's medals, but with glass Texaco goblets made by James Rush glassware manufacturers; James Rush was a Newcastle United director!

ME, JOHN TUDOR AND ALEX BRUCE WITH THE TEXACO CUP. THANK FUCK I FOUND A GOOD DENTIST

I never played against Steeley again in the next few seasons; all I knew was that Southampton won the FA cup in 1976 against a much fancied Manchester United with a goal scored by Bobby Stokes. That was the same year I spent the summer on loan to the Washington Diplomats in the USA.

In 1978 I returned to the States after signing a full time contract with the Diplomats. On my arrival, I was put up in the Washington National Airport Marriott Hotel for a couple of weeks until I had accommodation sorted out. I'd only been in my room for an hour or so when my telephone rang. I picked up the receiver and heard a deep Scottish voice on the other end. "Hey bruv, welcome back to DC. It's your mate Steeley. Did anyone tell you I'm the Dip's captain? I'll be over in half an hour and we'll go for a bevy." The first of thousands… We became great mates, drinking partners and the heart of the Dips.

STEELEY AND ME COMING OUT FOR THE SECOND HALF, I THINK HE'S STILL HOLDING A BUDWEISER!

Halfway through the season, we arrived in Florida to play the Tampa Bay Rowdies. After checking into The Bay Harbour Inn we went to the stadium for a practise session. We were met by none other than Gordon Hill who was running a soccer academy for the Rowdies called 'Soccer is a Kick in the Grass.' After training we had a beer with Gordon who found it ironic how Steeley and I had ended up great pals and here we were sitting at a table in Tampa with him having a beer. I asked him why he had looked so upset when he had sent Steeley off; it wasn't like he hadn't deserved it, he'd kicked me from pillar to post for over ninety minutes. "It's quite simple" he replied. "He," he said pointing at Steeley "is the only player I've ever sent off in my nine years in the professional game." He continued to explain that the yellow and red card disciplinary system had been new to him and he'd forgotten he'd already shown a yellow card to Steeley. He much preferred the old referee's notebook.

During his time as a referee, he had tried build closer relationships with the players and wanted to distance himself from the traditional image of a referee as an aloof disciplinarian. An approach that did not always find favour with the authorities. He even controversially admitted to swearing on the pitch which other officials, such as Pat Partridge, considered unwise for a referee, but Gordon felt it was natural behaviour for him and helped him communicate more effectively with the players on the pitch. Not something you'd expect from a head teacher from Leicester!

I wish there had been, or was now, more referees like Gordon Hill! Steeley and I continued to be bosom buddies, he kicked the other team's forwards and I clattered their goalkeepers.

I'll always remember our manager Gordon Bradley giving a pre-match team talk where he warned Steeley about the speed of our opponent's centre forward. "Danna worry" Steeley assured him, "They're all the same speed horizontal!" Nuff said…

27

I SEE A FULL MOON A RISING

Most soccer players gain sponsorship due to their ability, mine was due to my arse (with a bit of ability thrown in I hope).

I was into my second stint with the Washington Diplomats and enjoying considerable success. I'd scored a lot of goals and had received numerous yellow and red cards much to the delight of the fans but maybe not to the club officials.

We were playing at home in the fabulous RFK stadium on a Saturday evening, against the Tulsa Roughnecks. It had been a rough match, especially as I was being marked by Colin Waldron a typical old school English centre half who enjoyed being kicked almost as much as he enjoyed doing the kicking! Another ex pat on the Tulsa team was their goalkeeper, Colin Boulton, who I neatly placed, along with the ball, into the back of the net. I thought it was a perfectly good goal however the referee did not agree, disallowing it and showing me a yellow card in the bargain. I was more than a little upset and, to show my displeasure, I pulled my shorts down and did what I now know is a thing called 'mooning'.

I didn't think that much about it until I read the Washington Post the following day and was amazed to see a half page photograph of me 'mooning'. If that wasn't enough, it also appeared in an article about me in the world's best selling sports magazine, Sports Illustrated, some six weeks later. The North American Soccer League hierarchy were not amused and contacted the Diplomats with regards to banning me. As usual, we had the day off following a game and so it was on the Monday that I reported for training. I was summoned to see the general manager John Carbray, a man whose history was centred on baseball. Whilst I was waiting to see him, I overheard a conversation taking place in his office between him and Gordon Bradley, the Dips manager. Carbray was explaining to Bradley that the publicity my mooning had generated was worth hundreds of thousands of dollars; far more than would normally have been created by newspaper, radio and TV ads. It had lifted soccer onto the sports pages of every newspaper around the country. Seemingly, the league administrators were of the same opinion but they had to be seen to be doing something about it, they couldn't have players pulling their pants down 'willy nilly' and so I was to be suspended for two games and fined two weeks wages.

THE PICTURE THAT CAUSED AN UPROAR IN THE NASL. IT WAS TAKEN BY A PROFESSIONAL PHOTOGRAPHER'S SON WHO WAS IN THE CROWD. HIS NAME, JOHN PAUL RUPLENAS.

I went in to talk to Carbray who didn't realise I had overheard the entire conversation. He tried to justify my fine and the two game ban however, without being disrespectful, I laughed in his face, explaining that I had overheard the entire conversation he'd had with Bradley. His attitude changed immediately. He apologized and explained he had to comply with the league's edict but he would ensure that I would not lose out financially. I asked him how. He explained that the boss of Nike had been on the phone offering me a sponsorship deal. Seemingly he'd seen the article and the picture of me in Sports Illustrated and had asked "Why is this player not wearing Nike soccer shoes?", "Because we don't make white soccer shoes" was an underling's reply. "Well we do now" was the boss' retort! The rest, as they say, is history. I signed a contract with Nike that paid me well and all I had to do in return was to wear prototype white Nike soccer shoes, to give my feedback on their quality and suggest what, if any, modifications were necessary. From my experience, Nike were a superb outfit, they really looked after the players they had under contract and they tried to improve the quality of their products at every opportunity. I feel a tiny sense of pride when I see, after all these years, how Nike has become a major player in the soccer world.

It really seemed strange, at the time, wearing white football boots. The only player I had ever seen wearing them before was Newcastle United centre forward Wyn Davies who wore white Hummel boots. It's hard to believe when you see the huge selection of colours and materials available nowadays.

28

BLACK PUDDIN'

John Day was one of the die-hard regulars at the Sign O' the Whale. He'd been living in the States for around ten years but was originally from England. He was a high flyer with Rolls Royce but spent most of his time checking out women and sippin' Jack Daniels in the downtown DC bars.

It was the end of the 1980 season and I was on my way back to England for a few weeks. I was waiting for a taxi to pick me up from The Whale and take me to the airport. John remembered that I was on my way back to the UK so he asked me if I could bring something back for him. He knew my dad was a butcher and, as he couldn't get any decent black pudding in Washington, wondered whether I could I 'fix him up' with some. I felt like a black pudding dealer! Of course I agreed...

After a couple of weeks back in England I started me packing to return to the States. This included three beautiful shiny black puddings made by my dad's own fair hands. I checked me baggage in at Newcastle airport and thought no more about it until I landed at Washington's Dulles International Airport. I collected my luggage from the carousel and made my way to the customs and immigration desk. I've always hated clearing immigration since my first visit to D.C. in 1976. When the officers had checked my work visa it had me down as a professional footballer. Now, to the Americans, football means the NFL; a game played by huge steroid driven twenty stone animals hell bent on destroying each other, so they looked me up and down as though I was a fraud. "A bit weedy for a footballer ain't you sonny?" quipped one of the officers. "No wonder the Redskins are struggling". I eventually explained the difference between soccer and football and was allowed into the states with the officer still shaking his head!

Anyhoo, on this occasion, after clearing immigration I made my way to the customs desk where this huge black guy with a voice like gravel asked me the purpose of my journey; where I'd be staying, was I carrying any bombs, alcohol, tobacco, plants or foodstuffs. I answered no to all his questions, totally forgetting about the black puddings. "Can you open your bags for me sir?" asked the officer whom I duly and cheerfully obliged. After some time searching through my luggage, he eventually came across the three black puddings. "What are these sir?" he growled. Shit, I'd forgotten about them. "Oh sorry officer, I'd totally forgotten about them" I replied "they're black puddings". Now I don't know if he thought I was being racist towards him but his attitude got a lot nastier than it had started out. "And what are these 'puddings', they don't look like puddings to me". Gone was the 'sir' prefix. I could tell by the look on his face that he thought they contained drugs. "No they're not sweet puddings, they're savoury puddings, they're made of barley, fat and mostly pigs blood" I blurted out. Well I instantly knew he didn't believe me. He called for a fellow officer even bigger than him and I could see them in a huddle discussing the developing situation. They came back over to the desk, gloved up and armed with a Stanley knife and proceeded to split the three beautiful shiny black puddings open, revealing the pig's blood, the barley and the fat. The look of disgust on their faces was a treat. I actually thought that the biggest black bloke was going to hurl! "And you limey's really eat this shit?" he asked; "yes" I replied, "It's a Geordie delicacy".

Anyhoos, they ended up 'confiscating in order to destroy' the black puddings but only after donning fresh rubber gloves. John Day was gutted when he heard what had happened to his eagerly anticipated black puddings!

DO NOT TAKE BLACK PUDDINGS TO AMERICA; THEY WILL BE BRUTALLY ATTACKED AND TAKEN FROM YOU.

29

LORTON PRISON BLUES

The P.R. department did a brilliant job for the Washington Diplomats, coming up with many innovative projects and ideas to encourage the people of the local area to take an interest in soccer. They however, surpassed themselves when they sent us to Lorton Prison to do a soccer clinic! Lorton Prison was opened in 1916 as a facility for the more serious offenders in the Lorton Correctional Complex which in turn housed D.C's most violent prisoners (well apart from some women suffragettes years back). I always looked forward to doing soccer clinics; the kids were great and their parents were just as enthusiastic, always looking for tips that they could pass on to other members of the ever burgeoning soccer community. This clinic however, turned out to be slightly different.

When we had finished practice, we got changed into our soccer clinic uniforms; shorts, Diplomat shirts and trakkie tops. We then made our way to the reception area to be given our clinic schedule i.e. time of departure, driver name, time of arrival etc... oh, and the location of the clinic, in this case it read "Lorton Complex"....... No mention of the word 'correctional'!! Around ten of us set off in the team mini bus from R.F.K. en route to Lorton which was located in southern Fairfax County a good thirty minute or so's drive from D.C. During the drive, one of the players, Sonny Askew from Baltimore, commented that he was sure he'd heard of Lorton but he couldn't remember why. The driver of the bus, our P.R. guy Steve Rankin, chipped in with the answer...... it was a prison...a fuckin' prison! We were doing a soccer clinic for guy's doin' life!! He went on to explain that the session was fully booked; every prisoner who had been given the chance to participate had taken it. No fuckin' wonder; what would you rather do, get to run around in the open air playing soccer or stay stuck in a cell getting' rogered by a seven foot tall Cletus!

We eventually got to Lorton and were welcomed by a prison guard who was seemingly in charge of prisoner recreation....I was shit scared of him, never mind the inmates. We cleared security and were put in a tractor drawn trailer, to be taken over to the playing field where we'd be holding the clinic. As we rode through the prison, the inmates were shouting and screaming at us along with a chorus of wolf whistles which reached a crescendo as we passed the prison exercise yard. Little wonder, if you'd been banged up for years on end and a delivery of fit, fresh meat wearing nice, shiny short pants arrived, you'd think all your Christmas's had come early!

After running the gauntlet of sexual and racial abuse, we arrived at the practise field and we're 'unloaded' into the clutches of thirty of the biggest black blokes I'd ever seen. As I thought… they had not got the slightest clue about soccer; all they had wanted was to have a run around in the sunshine and to have a laugh at our expense! The clinic was a farce; the prisoners kept picking the ball up in their hands, tackling each other rugby style wherever the ball was and breaking away in small groups to have fights. Surprisingly, for such big hard blokes, they were terrified to head the ball. Anyway, we went through the motions for round about an hour or so, until Steve gave us a shout and told us to wind it up. I was just about to tell him what a waste of time this had been when he added insult to injury by reaching into his inside pocket and taking out a wad of tickets for our next home game, telling us to give them out to the prisoners that we thought had done well in the clinic!!! Fuckin' hell, they were lifers… as though they were going to be let out to join in the tailgate party, have a few beers and then watch the match; and, quite apart from that being fuckin' ludicrous, who would have had the guts to tell one of the prisoners that he couldn't have a 'get out of jail' ticket for the match as he hadn't paid enough attention during the clinic…. Not fuckin' me!!!

LORTON CORRECTIONAL COMPLEX. HEY WOULD YOU GUYS LIKE A GAME OF SOCCER? SURE AS LONG AS IT'S AWAY FROM HOME…

30

CH...CH...CH...CHANGES

The difference between playing for the Washington Diplomats on loan in 1976, to when I joined them permanently in 1978, was massive. The '76' Dips played at Woodson High School, the '78' Dips had the privilege of playing at the fabulous (at the time) RFK Stadium which we shared with the Washington Redskins, DC's American Football team. The stadiums were not the only difference. In 1976, the Diplomats were owned by Steve Danzansky and his father Joe who had made their fortunes via the 'Giant Supermarket' chain of stores. They were two smashin' guys but were not in, what you would call, the 'big league' when it came to American sports franchise ownership. When I returned in 1978, Danzansky was still team president but the actual owners were the Madison Square Garden Corporation under the leadership of the legendary Sonny Werblin. They, the Madison Square Garden Corporation, saw the future of soccer in pay per view and cable television channels; unfortunately, they were far too far ahead of their time and the idea failed, losing them some six million dollars in the process. However during the time they were in charge there was a remarkable difference in the players wearing the Diplomat shirt.

In the 1976 season, the Diplomats were composed mainly of ex British players that, and I don't think they'll mind me saying, were just a bit past their best before date. There were exceptions; Eric Martin, the ex Southampton goal keeper was still a class act, Roy Ellam an ex Leeds United centre half was still a force to be reckoned with and, with myself up front, we formed the spine of the team under the manager Dennis Viollet. I'll never forget my first game with the Dips. I had flown into Dallas alone to join the team but I was flying back to DC with them. I'd never seen anyone so nervous of flying as Dennis. I couldn't understand it; it seemed so irrational until Alan Spavin, the team captain, explained to me that Dennis was a survivor of the Manchester United Munich air disaster team... Fuckin' hell, no wonder he was so nervous! I had a lot of respect for Dennis, a great man. The rest of the team was made up of Canadians and Americans or should I say 'American citizens.' Mind you, this team really gelled. On the way to the playoffs we beat the New York Cosmos including Pele', I scored a couple of goals that game, as well as breaking the collar bone of the Cosmos and team USA goal keeper Bob Rigby. A sign of things to come?

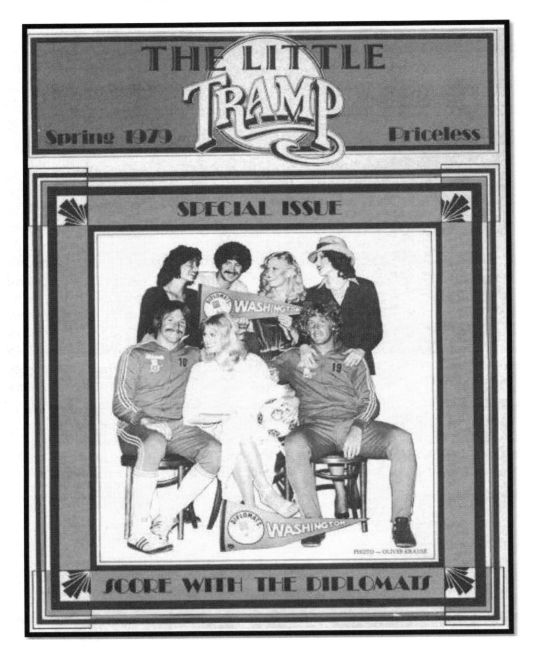

SOME THINGS NEVER CHANGE

THAT'S ME AT THE BACK (NOT RICHARD PRIOR!) BOB STETLER AND DON DROEGE AT THE FRONT DOING SOME INTENSE PRE SEASON TRAINING!

FUCKIN' HELL IT'S PAUL CANNELL

In comparison the 1978-9 Diplomat roster had players of real quality. Jim Steele ex Southampton and Rangers, the brilliant Johann Cruyff, Gus Hiddink, Bobby Stokes who scored Southampton's winning goal in the FA cup final against Manchester United and even Joe Horvath, a Hungarian international, who admitted to me that he had been terrified by the Leazes End fans when he played for Ujpest Dosza in the Inter Cities Fairs Cup final against Newcastle. Even the young American players had improved beyond all recognition.

As I've explained before, the 1976 team was managed by Dennis Viollet but the '78 team was managed by Gordon Bradley, the ex Cosmos boss, who was born in Easington Co. Durham in the North East of England. Gordon knew American soccer inside out and he, along with his second in command Joe Mallet, had a great rapport with both the players and the fans. They were both passionate about soccer and American soccer in particular.

Finally, one of the biggest differences between the '76 and the '78 seasons was the opposition! You would come up against players of genuine quality. Bobby Moore was playing for San Antonio, George Best for the L.A. Aztecs, Gerd Muller and Gordon Banks for the Fort Lauderdale Strikers and Franz Beckenbauer, Pele' and Giorgio Chinaglia (to name but a few) for the New York Cosmos. Maybe they were not at the peak of their careers but boy could they still play! I remember coming up against Beckenbauer at the Meadowlands Stadium, a game broadcast live on national television and I spent the entire ninety minutes of the match trying to kick him….. I could not get near him!

What a difference a season makes…

31

TOOT TOOT TOOTSIE... HELLO

During my time at Newcastle, my loan period in the states and after my return to the Toon, I'd never thought about hard drugs or had ever seen them around. However, when I left St James' for a permanent move to the Diplomats all that changed.

A couple of days after relocating to Washington DC, I went to a dinner party in Georgetown, the 'Chelsea' of the capital. I thought the evening was winding down until a public relations girl I knew from Tramps nightclub started chopping a white substance on our table right next to me. She split it carefully into lines and people took it in turns to snort it through a rolled up $100 bill. It came to my turn. "Do you want one Paul?" she asked. "What is it?" I asked. "Toot" she replied, "Go on everyone does it in Washington, I got this from a White House lawyer, it's really good stuff".

AND I MEAN <u>EVERYONE</u> WAS DOIN' COKE IN THOSE DAYS...

So, I thought; when in Rome... I sniffed the 'toot', and I didn't feel anything to start with, but I did get a quick slap when I put the rolled up $100 bill in my pocket! Well, shy bairns get now't. A few more lines followed and after moving on to Tramps nightclub and several visits to the toilet, I was feeling pretty good. Returning home, I had great difficulty sleeping. I eventually crashed out around six in the morning but I had to get up for training at eight. The alarm sounded and I got up feeling like shit. This was no hangover; I felt I'd woken up as a drug addict. On my way to training I simply couldn't get it out of my head that cocaine was a hard drug and once you'd taken it you were hooked. I felt dirty, guilty and sorry; my head was all over the place. I decided that I wasn't in a fit state to train and so I invented an ankle injury. As was the norm, I was sent to see the team's sports doctor, whose offices were ironically just up the road from Tramps.

As he examined my perfectly healthy ankle, I fired several guilt ridden questions at him. "What is cocaine exactly?", "Once you've taken it, does it make you an addict?", "What does it make you feel like?", "Do many people take it?" Eventually the doctor gave his prognosis on my injury. "I think you've got a slight ligament strain, nothing that a bit of ultrasound and cortisone won't cure. About the cocaine... would you like to try a line?"...

I loved Washington and I still do. I used to tell people in England that the D.C. in Washington D.C. stood for Different Class....... I now tell them it means Washington Does Coke!!!

32

THE MIGHTY QUINN

After my initial game in the North American Soccer League on the road in Dallas, the time had come for my home debut. The Dips played their home games at W.T. Woodson High School in Northern Virginia, the type of stadium you see in high school 'B' movies.

With a crowd of around 6,000, we beat, I think it was, Rochester 2-0; a good start to my Diplomat career. After the game, the crowd, I wouldn't exactly say "invaded" the pitch, they more or less walked on to it to talk to the players in a very casual manner. As this was only my second game for the Dips, I didn't expect anyone to come over to talk to me. However, on my way back to the locker room I felt a tap on my shoulder and I was confronted by a couple, brandishing a bottle of Newcastle Brown Ale! "Great game Paul" said this six foot odd bloke with a proper Geordie accent, "my name's Tony, Tony Quinn; I'm from Whitley Bay and this is my girlfriend Darlene!"

And so it came to pass... Tony was from Whitley Bay and he had a hairdressing salon in downtown D.C. We became good friends during my loan period in Washington and it was great to catch up with him again on my return in 1978.

When I did return, after signing for the Diplomats permanently, we picked up our friendship; me playing soccer, him cutting hair. Now if you haven't been to the States you won't realise what the humidity is like in the summer months. It played havoc with me 'wig'. I'd always had long straight hair and it was a pain in the arse to sort it out after having a shower. Tony, being a high class D.C. coiffure suggested I had a curly perm because it would handle the humidity better and it would be much easier to look after. For some months I put it off, I was a Geordie lad and we didn't do girly curls. However, after much persuasion, I gave in and agreed to go under the perm solution. My appointment was at 3pm. After training, Jim Steele and I went to the Sign O' the Whale bar at 1pm as was the daily ritual. I decided I needed a lot of alcoholic persuasion in order to go through with this 'lifestyle change'. By 2.45pm I was totally pissed. I staggered the two blocks to Tony's studio thinking "a perm, ah what the hell".

My time in the chair was a bit of a blur, Tony did his thing, and I left and went back to the Whale with my new hairstyle. My reception was predictable.

FUCKIN' HELL IT'S PAUL CANNELL

The regulars, all my pals, took the piss relentlessly. My reaction was what was normal for me at the time, alcohol, cocaine, Quaaludes and more alcohol. I was eventually bundled into a taxi at midnight and sent home.

I couldn't remember going to bed, but I do remember vividly waking up with a huge hangover in the morning. I realised that I'd missed training but I couldn't understand what this horrible, cat's piss-like stench, was in the bedroom. I staggered into the bathroom to brush my teeth and looked in the mirror, recoiling and gasping in horror to see this Richard Prior lookalike staring right back at me! I mean my hair was bigger than all Five of the Jackson's put together! In my drunken state I'd totally forgotten that I'd had my hair permed. I did however see the funny side of it and I've remained good friends with Tony to this day.

FUCKIN' HELL, IT'S CURLY CANNELL!

Photography was a hobby for Tony so Jim Steele and I fixed him up with a press/photography pass that enabled him to take pitch side photos during games. His photography skills developed to such an extent that he ended up (and still is) the USA soccer team's official photographer; he also works for the US

79

Olympic teams and the current professional soccer team in Washington, D.C. United. He is, not only a great talent behind the hairdryer but also behind the lens!

33

THE PRESIDENT'S DAUGHTER

During my first stint on loan to the Washington Diplomats, I was introduced to Georgetown, the party area of Washington and the hottest spot in town, Winston's. This was one of the venues that you needed to be known to get in. Fortunately I knew people that were known, so I became known and got in!

One Saturday night in Winston's, after a game and with me off me face as usual, I spotted this attractive girl who seemed to be the centre of attention. Full of alcoholic and chemical bravado I sauntered, well staggered over and asked if her if she wanted to dance. To everyone's amazement she said yes! We had a few dances then sat down at a table and had a few drinks. I could see that people were talking and pointing at us but when you are trying to pull, well you don't really give a shit. As the club was closing, I asked her if she wanted to go for a meal on Wednesday. She said she wasn't certain about the meal (I said it would be meat!) but that she'd see me in Winston's and we could take it from there. I left and yes, no lectures about drinking and driving please, I drove home to Reston, Virginia and thought no more about it. The following day I got a phone call from the Diplomat's PR girl. "What the hell were you doing last night at Winston's?" she asked. "Nowt special" I replied. "Well I think you were trying to 'do' the president's daughter" she replied. Then, all of a sudden, it came back to me; her name was Susan (Ford) and all of her associates were wearing black suits and dark glasses and they didn't look very happy that she was hanging out with me!

On the Monday, I received a phone call, this time from the Washington Star newspaper, informing me that Diana Mclellan had heard about our rendezvous and it would be appearing in one of America's biggest gossip columns 'The Ear' and, as a result of that, I would be sent a gold tie pin in the shape of an ear to commemorate the event!

Anyways, I got the piss taken out of me relentlessly by the rest of the team and they all promised (or threatened would be a better word) to be in Winston's on Wednesday night.

The phone never stopped, everyone wanting to know what was going on and so, by the Wednesday, the last thing I wanted to do was to go to Winston's. I was afraid that you couldn't get more publically stood up than that. When I turned up on the night, she was already there; we had a couple of drinks then went to a restaurant opposite Winston's called Le Fillet. However it's not the same when you are sober and surrounded by dark glassed, gun toting men (by the way, can you explain to me why they have 'Secret Service' emblazoned on their cars?). We had a meal, made some small talk then she made some excuse and left to join her friends. I even paid! I never saw her again…not even in Georgetown… but it was a few days to remember!

SUSAN FORD
I WAS SO PISSED I THOUGHT THAT I WAS SEEING TREBLES!!!

34

I'M WAITING FOR MY MAN...

Joe was a drug dealer and not a very good one at that; he gave away as much as he sold. He was also very different from your normal dealer who would try to be inconspicuous; Joe might as well have had a neon sign on his head flashing "I SELL DRUGS". He was 6ft 3 inches tall, had a pockmarked face, beard, Stetson, string tie and cowboy boots and yes, he drove a pink Cadillac with a fur dashboard and hanging furry dice. But he was a great guy. We'd met him in the Sign O' the Whale (me and some of the other players) and had got talking. We had mutual interests, he was into soccer and we were into cocaine! We got him tickets for the home games and he became a regular at post game parties. He often used to bring his girlfriend to the games; we had recognised her as she was a pole dancer in King Arthurs, a joint next to the Whale. Joe was always grateful for his match tickets, so much so that he invited me to one of his 'business' parties. I was to meet him at 1a.m. outside King Arthurs and he'd drive us to the shin dig. "Why so late" I asked him, "hey, my guys work late hours, oh, did I mention it? The party is in Ocean City!" a good few hours' drive from DC. I met him and his girlfriend outside the club and we set off in his lurid 'Caddy' en route to Ocean City.

DEALER JOE'S INCONSPICUOUS RUN AROUND...

FUCKIN' HELL IT'S PAUL CANNELL

"We're here" announced Joe, shaking me as I was slumped asleep in the back seat. The sun was rising over Ocean City. "What time is it?" I asked. "About six o'clock" he replied. "They'll just be getting started". We walked through a front door that was wide open and into a classy beach front house full of, what I was later to find out, the east coast's finest drug dealers! Joe wasn't such an insignificant guy after all. It was so strange to be at a party where the drugs were not done in the toilet; people were swapping samples of cocaine and discussing prices, quantities, effects and quality, and it was all free!!!

Joe disappeared for a while. I realised, by now, it was around lunch time and I needed to get home so I went to look for him. I found him in the conservatory playing backgammon blindfolded! He lost the game and seemingly lost £10k. We decided to hit the road back to DC. Cocaine keeps you alert but it doesn't enable you to see in the dark.

It had been quite an experience at Joe's 'works do' so I decided to repay the compliment. I'd been invited to the premiere of Evita at Washington's National Theatre and I had a spare ticket. We'd booked a limo and had arranged to leave from the Sign O' the Whale at 6.30pm. Joe was over the moon, doing gigs like that, as he put it, made him feel normal. We (the ones going to the theatre) were all having pre show drinks in the Whale, all looking very dapper, the men in our penguin suits and the ladies in their cocktail dresses when suddenly a pink Caddy pulled up outside, it's horn blaring. I looked out of the window and saw Joe beckoning me to come outside. Everyone was looking on as I left the bar and got into his car. He screeched off immediately, throwing me back in the passenger seat. He was driving like a mad man. "Paul, you gotta' look at this" he said as he thrust a Petri dish into my lap. "It's fabulous, pink Peruvian flake, the best coke you can get, try a bit but hurry up, we're being followed." I didn't need to be asked twice, I opened the Petri dish and took a pinch of this pink powder but, before I could get it to my nose, he threw the car around a corner and the dish flipped over on my lap, spilling its contents all over me. "Jesus Christ" he gasped as he slammed on the brakes in the middle of a very busy M Street. We both started to scrape the cocaine off my lap and back into the Petri dish. "Shit, there's five grand's worth still on your fucking crotch" he moaned. "Never mind that, you paranoid fucker" I replied "get back to the Whale, we've got a premiere to go to oh, and by the way, there are two fuckin' cop cars stuck in the traffic behind you!" That did not help his paranoia… or his driving skills.

THIS IS WHAT COKE LOOKS LIKE IF YOU'VE NEVER DONE IT...

We eventually got back to the bar and Joe wisely decided that he'd give the premiere a miss. I had to explain to the rest of the gang why I'd been kidnapped by a maniac in a pimp-mobile then returned covered in pink sherbet!!!

35

COME ON OVER TO MY PLACE

We'd just played the Tulsa Roughnecks at RFK Stadium and the post game party was coming to an end. The Tulsa players had the use of hire cars as they were not leaving DC for a couple of days because they were on a three game road trip. Jim Steele and the rest of the Dips, along with most of the Tulsa players and 'invited guests', decided the party should continue at my place as I lived the closest. I must have been drunk as I agreed!

We were all pissed as we got into our cars and set off in a convoy to my place with me leading the way, Steeley was tailgating and the rest following behind. I kept looking in my rear view mirror to check if they were still following. These cars headlights kept getting closer and closer to me. Thinking it was Steeley who was a mad driver, I accelerated to keep well clear but the headlights seemed to keep getting closer the faster I went until I eventually got outside my apartment building and realised Steeley didn't have flashing lights on the top of his car. Unfortunately for me, it was the cops I'd been doing a runner from! The officer came up to my car and asked me to get out, onto the sidewalk. That's when I should have sobered up, but no, I'd had far too much to drink and instead of opening my driver's door and stepping out onto the sidewalk, I fell over the door as I had the top and windows down on my Vette. I stumbled to my feet; the cop just looked at me with incredulity. He cautioned me, saying he was arresting me for driving while intoxicated and he asked the girl, who I'd been giving a lift to, if she could get my car off the road. She was drunker than me! The last I saw of me Vette was it kangaroo-bouncing towards my apartment, whilst I was en route to a Virginia lock up.

On my arrival I was thrown into a holding cell full of drug dealers and pimps (and I didn't recognize a single one of them!). I sat in the corner waiting for my mates to come and get me out as I knew they must have seen the whole incident. After a couple of hours I realised my 'knights in shining armour' were not turning up and so I shouted to the desk sergeant if I could make a phone call to the only number I could remember… my own. I don't remember whether I was pissed off or pleased when Steeley answered my phone. "Hey bruv, where are you?" he asked above a cacophony of noise "I'm in fuckin' Alexandria jail ya twat" I replied. I'd totally forgotten that I had given him a key for my condo in case of emergencies which is just as well otherwise nobody would have answered the phone. "Hey I'll get a cab and get you out as soon as possible" promised Steeley. Well, his idea of 'as soon as possible' was definitely not my idea of 'as soon as possible'. By six in the morning I realised nobody was turning up. The cops eventually got me a Rastafarian bail bondsmen who put up the $5,000 bail and gave me a lift home. I brayed on my front door for several minutes until this dishevelled drunk opened it. When I got in I found bodies lying everywhere but not a sign of Steeley!

As a result of my DWI conviction I wasn't banned from driving immediately, however I was instructed to attend an alcohol awareness programme but before I had a chance to attend one, I'd moved to Memphis. The American system is quite flexible, rather than taking a fresh driving test to get a Tennessee license, I enrolled in one of their alcohol awareness programmes which would simply enable me to continue driving on my Virginian license. The course... I've never seen anything like it! It was held in a downtown Memphis office building. I was the only white person there and I was the only one vaguely sober. The rest of the 'students' were either high as kites or pissed out of their brains and they'd all driven there! After three weeks, the course teacher was still trying to explain to his students that a bottle of moonshine counted as more than one unit of alcohol and, at the end of the course, the 'graduates' were all convinced that they were now entitled to drink and drive as they'd completed the programme successfully!

36

UNDER THE KNIFE

Towards the end of the 1979 season, I started to miss games due to an injury to my left shin (well it made a change from missing games due to red cards). I had developed a habit of blocking tackles with my left leg (I didn't use it for much else) and the pain was getting worse. At the end of the season I returned to England for a couple of weeks where I went to see an orthopaedic surgeon that Newcastle had used, a Dr Stephenson.

He took a scan of the area and concluded that I had a 'hot spot'. Seemingly I'd been kicked so often in the same area that, instead of the usual bruising, my body was producing calcium between the tibia and fibula bones forming a plate joining the two bones together. This plate was splitting through the muscles of my lower leg causing all the pain. He said he couldn't do the operation right now as the bone formation wasn't complete and the process would simply start again. I would have to wait, return to America and get another scan to see if the hot spot had cooled down and the bone formation was complete. The bone joining the fibula and tibia could then be chiselled out, relieving the pain. It sounded simple; however he didn't know who would be doing the operation in Washington!

Carl McArtee, the Diplomat's sports doctor was a great bloke, a brilliant surgeon, but as barmy as a bucket of frogs. He used to party with us regularly, especially on a Tuesday night in Chadwick's of Georgetown.

I returned to DC and explained the situation to Gordon Bradley and to Carl. The Dips were due to travel to Korea (Bradley loved the Koreans, they had a work ethic he admired) for a pre season tour. It was agreed that if the bone growth was complete, I would have the surgery immediately and recuperate whilst the rest of the team were in Korea. As I would be unable to walk after the operation, I would have to stay in the Hyatt Hotel in Roslyn as I wouldn't be unable to look after myself at home in Alexandria. I had a second scan, which confirmed that the bone growth was complete, so the operation was scheduled.

The team left for Korea and they all wished me well for my surgery (we really did have a smashing bunch of players). I was really envious of them as I knew for a fact that they would have a great time in the Far East. They checked into Dulles airport and I checked into Georgetown hospital. Once I was tucked up in bed I was visited by the anaesthetist who explained I could either have a general anaesthetic or an epidural. It was up to me but he said there was no hurry as Carl McArtee was coming in to see me later that day. Carl arrived a couple of hours later, explained about the following day's procedure, then apologized that he had to leave as he was starting early at Chadwick's... I'd forgotten it was Tuesday! I spent the rest of the afternoon and that evening wondering what kind of state the guy who was operating on me the following day was going to get into and more importantly, what would he be like the following morning as my surgery was scheduled for 10am.

I woke up on Wednesday morning feeling very nervous; I'm not a lover of hospitals, needles or pain. I was given something meant to relax me, a pre op or something and I was feeling pretty woozy as I was wheeled down to the operating theatre. I was parked up in the corridor, just outside the operating theatre, for what seemed like ages. I overheard a couple of 'gowned up' theatre nurses commenting on how Carl was running late and they were wondering how long he'd be. More time passed until I suddenly heard the doors behind me opening and a head, sporting a deer stalker hat, suddenly appeared above me. I half sat up and realised it was Carl and in his mouth was a Sherlock Holmes style pipe. "Sorry I'm late" he apologized "late one at Chadwick's" I flopped back down on the trolley. Things didn't look good. He was holding a Polaroid style camera and asked me if I wanted some memories of the surgery. He also asked me whether I wanted to be knocked out for the duration of the operation or would I like to be awake as I might find it interesting! As I remember fuck all after that, you can guess which option I chose.

CHADWICKS OF GEORGETOWN, THEY SEEMINGLY DO PRE-OPS!

FUCKIN' HELL IT'S PAUL CANNELL

I woke up some hours later to find Carl sitting by my bedside. I didn't really know whether it was to give me a medical update or if he was still recovering from the previous night. He said the procedure had gone well and that I was to begin recuperation within twenty four hours. My left leg was in plaster from my toes to my thigh. I was discharged the following day and taken by taxi to the Hyatt Hotel. I spent the next few weeks alone there, living like a king. I signed for everything, food, drink, and even porn channels. To give the Diplomats their due I wanted for nothing. The physios came every day to make sure I was doing my post op exercises which, I must admit, I found very hard to do as the pain was so severe. It felt like my leg was going to explode, it was agony. By the time the team returned from Korea, the plaster had been removed and I was able to begin light training. Although I was deemed fully fit by the start of the season, I never felt totally confident with my left leg again. My form suffered and when Memphis came in to sign me I jumped at the chance as I thought a change of scene, a new challenge and new medical staff would be just the boost I needed.

I was never the player I was but I could never put my finger on a specific reason why. I felt I was running differently, I definitely stopped blocking tackles with my left leg and I just didn't seem to be able to jump as well as I had before the operation. The reason became clear after an unexpected telephone call. I was with Bob Stetler in my apartment in Memphis when the phone rang; Stetz answered it and handed the phone to me saying it was a bloke from some insurance company. I was about to say to him that I didn't want to buy anything however I quickly became interested in what he had to say. He wanted to confirm my new address as he had a cheque for $7,000 for me. It was medical compensation as I'd seemingly lost 15% of the movement of my big toe due to the operation. At least I now knew the reason why I'd never be the same player again.

37

I WAS WALKIN' IN MEMPHIS

It was my third day in Memphis and after training, I was asked to pop into the club's offices to meet their PR girl, whose name escapes me. At the meeting she explained that I needed to live up to my image in Memphis, to be what they had bought, a player with a bad guy reputation! She arranged to pick me up at midnight that night and we'd cruise the bars and night clubs; now that was my kind of training!

We started the evening off at TGI Fridays in Overton Square, nipped over to the BBC (the Bombay Bicycle Club) headed down to No 1 Beale Street, hit another couple of bars downtown, then headed over to the Élan nightclub and finally on to Cowboys, a club popular with the country music crowd. I was talking to a few people at the bar when the PR girl came up to me. "I'd like to introduce you to someone" she said, and dragged me over to a table in the VIP area. There were about ten people sitting around this table with bottles of Scotch and vodka in front of just about every one of them. "Paul" she said "I'd like to introduce you to one of Memphis' finest, Mr Jerry Lee Lewis". Jerry stood up and shook my hand with a very firm grip. "Nice to meet you son" he drawled "I've read about you. I don't understand much about this soccer thing, but I sure do appreciate someone who gets into trouble a lot". His cronies and the PR girl burst into what seemed like arse licking laughter. "Sit down" Jerry ordered; I obeyed! After some inane chit chat he asked me where exactly it was in England that I came from (I guess either my accent made it obvious or he had read about me in the papers. I think the former was more likely). "Newcastle on Tyne" I replied. "Newcastle upon Tyne" mused Jerry emphasising the up in upon. "Dave, where are we playing in Newcastle upon Tyne on our next tour?" "The Mayfair" replied Dave, who I later found out was his tour manager. "Well if yer' back home when we play there, come on down and we'll have some fun!" I thanked him for the offer and after a couple of Scotch shooters (I hate Scotch) me and the PR girl left to hit the Quilted Camel and another couple of bars. At around 3am, we decided to head home. On our drive back to Germantown, where I lived, we had to pass Cowboys which was still open. "Howay" I said "Let's have one for the ditch." "Don't you mean for the road?" asked the PR girl "Listen" I said "If I were driving it would be the fuckin' ditch!" On reaching the bar at Cowboys,

91

even though it was late, we noticed how quiet it was. "Where's Jerry Lee Lewis gone?" I asked the waitress. "Oh he got drunk and punched a bar tender" I was told "nothing unusual!"

The following day was a day off so I decided to have a wander around the Overton Square area and go and see a few sights. I popped into the Sun Recording studios on Union Avenue where Elvis and Johnny Cash made their names, had a walk around Audubon Park then, as usual, ended up in TGI Fridays for a few beers and lunch. I then decided to hit a bar just down the road from the BBC that featured live artists and during the day had a 'go as you please.' There were only about a dozen people in the bar when I arrived. There was a small stage in the far corner of the room, with a mike and a high stool. I sat at the bar making small talk with the barman and eating popcorn. There was, what I considered, a slightly scruffy looking bloke sat at the far end of the bar who appeared to be talking to his drink. I thought he was pissed. After a few minutes he picked up his guitar and made his way to the stage. I thought it was going to be a disaster but he broke into a brilliant version of Polk Salad Annie, a huge hit for Elvis Presley I believe. "Bloody Hell" I said to the barkeep "he's fuckin magic" "so he should be" he replied "It's Tony Joe White, he wrote the damn song!"

The Who were playing the South West Coliseum indoor arena and, as we played our indoor soccer games there, we knew the arena manager who kindly provided me and Bob Stetler with two tickets in return for a soccer lesson for his two sons (There is no such thing as a free lunch).

After training, on the day of the concert, Stetz and I set about getting into the mood. We hit all the bars in Overton Square then purchased a quarter of an ounce of toot as well as a bottle of vodka and a bottle of coke which we hid in a Piggly Wiggly supermarket bag!

The Who were fantastic… playing all their hits to a sell out crowd both in the auditorium and in the toilets. For some unknown reason, nobody was taking a piss; they all seemingly wanted to use the cubicles. It took about an hour to gain access to a crapper so when we eventually got in one, we snorted several lines each as we realised it would be quite a while before we'd get another one. By the time we got back to our seats, the show was almost over… but by that time we didn't really care. We were just about to finish the vodka when we were 'arrested' by the arena security guards for public drinking oh, and for some reason, Stetz had pulled his pants doon which they were also not too happy aboot! We missed the end of the concert as we were getting 'booked' however by the time we were released, the parking lot had cleared so, in our sozzled state, we found it easy to find me motor!

FUCKIN' HELL IT'S PAUL CANNELL

Stetz had come in my car as it was pointless both of us getting done for DWI, (drunk driving in English). I drove very carefully down Union Avenue and had just passed the Rogues' offices when I heard sirens. I looked in the rear view mirror and saw flashing lights, the cops! I pulled in as quickly as I could and wound down the window. Thinking quickly, I was doing everything quickly, I threw the still half full packet of coke over the top of the car before the cops could get to us. One got out of the cop car and approached. He leaned down to the low Corvette and told us not to make any sudden movements. He asked if we had been drinking which we admitted as we stunk of booze. I'd rather be done for drink than coke… "Hey" he said "Do you guys play for the Rogues?" (Very quick, saying we were both wearing Rogues jackets and had a Rogues parking permit on the windscreen). "My kids love soccer and never miss a game. Can I see your license?" Fortunately I had taken my state driving test and had obtained a Tennessee license which I took out of my wallet and handed to him. "So, you live in Germantown huh? Listen, it's only a couple of miles down the road, follow me but don't get too close!" We took off behind him, sirens wailing and lights flashing, a police escort home!

Two Rogues Arrested At Concert

Two Memphis Rogues soccer players were arrested last night at The Who concert at the Mid-South Coliseum — one accused of dropping his pants and the other of being disorderly.

Bob Stetler, a Rogues goalkeeper, was charged with open and notorious public lewdness and public drunkenness. An arrest report said a private security guard saw Stetler "standing in front of his seat with his pants down exposing himself."

Rogues forward Paul Cannell was charged with disorderly conduct and public drunkenness. The arrest report on him quoted a security guard as saying Cannell banged on a glass door and threw a soft drink bottle at guards when they asked him to stop.

Both players are to be in City Court Division 7 at 9 a.m. today.

In separate incidents, one youth was arrested in the Coliseum and two men were arrested at Airways and Scottswood, all charged with attempting to sell T-shirts without permits. Several other T-shirt sellers were not arrested, and Lt. B. W. Nelson said City Councilman Oscar H. Edmonds Jr. questioned police about why they weren't. Nelson said he explained they had peddler's permits. *6-11-80*

IT WAS SUPPOSED TO BE ME WHO DROPPED ME PANTS

THANK GOD ITS FRIDAYS... WE GOT SHIT FACED THERE ON SATURDAYS, SUNDAYS, MONDAYS, TUESDAYS, WEDNESDAYS AND THURSDAYS AS WELL!

When we woke up in the morning, (Stetz had crashed out on me sofa) we realised how lucky we had been; however we'd still lost a couple of hundred bucks worth of toot. On the way to training we stopped off en route and started searching the area where we had thrown the packet of coke out of the car. It was dead busy as it was rush hour. We couldn't find the packet so we returned to my car. We were just about to drive off when we heard a tap on the window. It was the same cop from the night before! Talk about déjà vu! I wound the window down wondering what the hell he wanted.

The officer lowered his head into the Vette and asked "Is this what you've been looking for?" holding up a half empty packet of white powder. Before I could reply, he emptied the contents onto the ground and said "Don't be so stupid in future, this stuff is dangerous, oh and by the way, good luck for the game at the weekend..." Stetz and I looked at each other in total disbelief then slowly merged into the early morning traffic and made our way to training. There are some good cops!

38

HAVE YOU SEEN THE COOKIE MAN?

TELL YOUR KIDS NEVER TO ACCEPT COOKIES FROM A STRANGER...ESPECIALLY IN MEMPHIS!!

When the Memphis Rogues returned from a road trip, they were always welcomed home, at the airport, by the Booster Club; a crowd of about fifty fanatical supporters. One of them had always intrigued me. He had the nickname of the 'Cookie Man' which had something, I presumed, to do with Charlie Cooke the Rogues manager. This fan was very popular, he always had a large congregation around him, but I'd never known why. That was all to change one afternoon when we returned from a six day road trip to the west coast.

Upon landing and collecting our luggage from the carousel (damaged as usual...you'll find out why later) we emerged through the arrival doors to be greeted, as usual, by the Booster Club. I'd had a good trip scoring a couple of goals and several assists so I wasn't too surprised when the Cookie Man came over and congratulated me. He then offered me what looked like and what I believed to be, a Maryland chocolate chip cookie. As it had been a while since we'd had our in-flight meal, I readily accepted it. It tasted good and like a typical greedy Geordie I asked him if he had another one. "Can I have some more please sir?" I should have realised all was not as it seemed by his slightly surprised look; however he reached into his bag and produced another of his cookies. The cookie man seemed a lovely bloke…

We left the arrival terminal and I jumped into my parked car and proceeded to make my way, as we always did after a road trip, to TGI Fridays in Overton Square. I had great difficulty getting the key into the car door and even greater difficulty remembering how the car started. When I eventually got the thing moving, I couldn't remember where the hell I was meant to be going. It took me an hour to get to Fridays, where I had been on numerous occasions, a journey that should normally have taken less than fifteen minutes; I mean even bicycles were overtaking me! When I eventually arrived at the bar, I was greeted by the rest of the team and a group of supporters to a rousing chorus of "now you know the cookie man, the cookie man, the cookie man" sung to the tune of the well-known kids' song 'Have you seen the Muffin Man.' I think his cookies contained something called marijuana. I've never touched a Maryland cookie since. Oh, and it took me two bloody days to find my car!!!

39

DEAL OR NO DEAL... THAT IS THE QUESTION

Memphis was a magic place, the phrase 'sex and drugs and rock and roll' was surely invented there. The music of Beale Street, the nightlife of Overton Square and the ghost of Elvis had all been put in a pot and blended with a pinch of 'the beautiful game' to form a new soccer franchise called the Memphis Rogues. It was very fitting that their offices were just down the road from the iconic Sun Recording Studios.

At the time, I was under contract with Nike Sportswear and received a payment every six months or so. This had been negotiated through my agent, a gentleman called Ken Adam, a Brit who had set up the football magazine 'Shoot' in the U.K. or so I was told. He was now based in New York but lived in Ft. Lauderdale; he also had Jim Steele and George Best on his books. Ken rang me and explained that when Nike sent me a payment they had to deduct taxes etc. Now he, being a very astute representative, had found a way to 'avoid' paying that tax. He suggested that the cheque should be made payable to him, he would sort out the tax and then he would send me the balance in, cocaine! I liked the idea. An ounce or so of coke every six months, cut down, sold, I would realise $6,000 every three months instead of $300 and no taxes! A no brainer except it was slightly illegal. Not a problem. Well at least that's what I thought.

My next Nike payment was due. Ken rang me to say that the cheque had cleared and he was sending my 'payment' that day. That's when the alarm bells started ringing. A little while later I rang Ken back to ask him how I was to get the coke. "No need to worry" was his reply. "I've already sent it; by Federal Express, it'll be there tomorrow..." "What? To my address?" I asked in a panic. "No I'm not that stupid" he replied. "You'll have to pick it up from the Federal Express depot at the airport; it's down as soccer shoes on the label."

Well, apart from the fact that I was terrified of picking up an ounce of cocaine from anywhere, there was the added snag that it was from the Fed Ex building in Memphis and Fred Smith, the owner of Fed Ex, had also been involved in the ownership of the Rogues. It was almost surreal. What should I do? The answer, Stetz!

FUCKIN' HELL IT'S PAUL CANNELL

We finished training and Stetz and I went, as usual, for a couple of drinks to TGI Fridays in Overton Square. After an hour or so, I asked him if he could pick up some new soccer shoes... Oops I've had an Uncle Sam moment... I mean football boots... that Nike had sent me to test. I couldn't collect them because I had to call into the Rogues offices. "No problem bro' " was his reply; I gave him my I.D. and off he went. I drove home feeling a bit shitty about putting him in that position but I was thinking positively, everything would go to plan. At least the package was in my name so that if anything did happen, it would come down on my toes not his... but at least I'd be arrested at home!

I got back around 4pm. 5pm passed, 6pm, 7pm; now I'm starting to get worried. I'm thinking the worst. 8pm and my door opens and there's Stetz, absolutely off his fucking face. "Shit bro'- shit bro' man shit bro'" he gabbled like some deranged chipmunk "can you get me a fuckin' sponsorship deal like yours?" Obviously, curiosity had gotten the better of him and he'd just had to have a sneaky look inside the package to see what kind of new boots I was getting! I decided that the trauma involved in picking up the cocaine shipment definitely wasn't worth the couple of hundred dollars I was saving in taxes; that was quite apart from the fact that I never sold any of it and me, Stetz and Steeley were totally wired for a week. Thank God Stetz could get Quaaludes cheap to get some kip!!!

ENDORSEMENT AGREEMENT

AGREEMENT, made this ___First___ day of ___September,_____, 1978, between
PAUL CANNELL_____ ("PLAYER"), and BRS, Inc ("BRS").
c/o ADAM MANAGEMENT CORP

1. PLAYER TO WEAR NIKE SHOES. During the term of this Agreement, PLAYER
   will wear NIKE shoes during all practices and games and all other
   occasions in which he wears his soccer uniform or plays soccer; at all
   soccer or sports camps or clinics and all occasions in which he is
   engaged in soccer or athletic (such as "Superstars") promotional
   activities.

2. OTHER AGREEMENTS. During the term of this Agreement, PLAYER will not:
   A. Sponsor, endorse or wear any athletic shoe sold by any manufacturer
      and/or seller other than BRS, or
   B. enter into any endorsement or promotional agreement with any other
      manufacturer and/or seller of athletic shoes.

3. PAYMENTS. BRS shall pay PLAYER: BONUS PAYMENTS:
   A. $ 500 __ by September 1, 1978 $250 on September 1, 1979
   B. $ 500 __ by March 31, 1979 $500 on September 1, 1980
   C. $ 1000 _ by September 1, 1979 $500 selection for NASL 1st Team
   D. $ 1000 _ by March 31, 1980 $250 selection for NASL 2nd Team
                                           $100 selection for NASL 3rd Team

4. TERM. This Agreement shall remain in full force and effect from the —
   date of execution until September 1st, 1980.

5. TERMINATION. BRS may terminate this Agreement if, at any time during
   the term of this Agreement:
   A. During the NASL regular and/or playoff season and the Football
      League season PLAYER fails for a period of eight (8) consecutive
      weeks to play in an NASL or Football League professional Soccer
      match, or
   B. PLAYER fails to perform any of his other obligations or duties
      provided under this Agreement.

_____   _____

PLAYER   BRS, Inc
                                           Tony Penman, NIKE Soccer Coach

MY NIKE AGREEMENT

ΛM

ADAM MANAGEMENT LTD
9 HILLGATE STREET
LONDON W8 7SP
Telephone: 01- 727 2791/4
Telex: 25728 Sunarts

ADAM MANAGEMENT CORPORATION
130 WEST 57th STREET
SUITE 6D, NEW YORK, NY 10019
Telephone: 212-765 7550
Telex: 420991 Sirr

AGREEMENT

made this 15 day of January,   1979 between PAUL CANNELL
of 47 Stanley Grove, High Heaton, Newcastle-on-Tyne
(hereinafter refered to as "The Player") and KEN ADAM of Adam
Management Corporation, Suite 201, 112 Central Park South,
New York, N.Y. 10019 (hereinafter refered to as "The Agent")

Whereby:

1. The Player appoints the Agent as his exclusive representative
    for a period of three years from the date of the signing of
    this agreement.

2. The Player agrees that The Agent shall negotiate all contracts
    on his behalf with his employers, whoever they may be, during
    the period of the agreement.

3. In consideration of clause two above, The Player agrees to
    pay the Agent a commission of Ten   per cent on all salaries,
    bonuses and signing-on fees negotiated by The Agent. above
    $25,500 per annum

Signed:

PAUL CANNELL

Signed:

KEN ADAM

Registered in England No. 1150896
Registered Office: 23 Albemarle Street London W1Y 4DB

Please reply to:

MY AGENT AGREEMENT

OH AYE, I FORGOT ABOUT THIS AGREEMENT!

40

CREAKING FLOORBOARDS

I'd been seeing this girl on and off for a few weeks, I'd met her in TGI Fridays and we got on really well. There was nothing serious about it, she drank with her friends, I drank with her friends, my friends and anyone else's friends I could drink with!

One Saturday night after a game, we decided in a drunken stupor to go back to her place. I only realised when we got there that I had never been to her house. After a few drinks and a bit fooling around, we were both naked on her sofa. Suddenly, we heard the sound of a car door slamming which seemed to surprise her for some reason. She leapt to her feet, ran over to the window and peeked through the blinds. "Christ, it's my husband!" she exclaimed. "You're fuckin' husband! You never said anything about a fuckin' husband!" I stammered."Hurry up" she continued "he's a baggage handler at Memphis airport so he's used to throwing things around and damaging them" Fuckin' great I thought as she picked up my clothes and stuffed them behind the sofa. "Get upstairs" she ordered "and whatever you hear, do not, I repeat, do not come down until I come up and tell you that it's safe!" Well I didn't need to be told twice; I shot up the stairs like an Olympic sprinter and hid in one of the bedrooms. I heard the key in the door, the door opening, then closing and then raised voices. I was stood in a strange bedroom, bollock naked, bloody freezin' and shittin' meself. I heard what sounded like a fight... the sound of glass breaking. I tried to move but the floorboards creaked like hell. Then there was silence. I thought about going downstairs but I remembered all too well what I had been told; plus, I thought, he might have a gun; after all, most of the southerners I'd met, had more guns than kids! I stood in the same position for the longest twenty fuckin' minutes of my life, terrified to move. Eventually, I heard footsteps coming up the stairs. Fuckin' hell I thought, was it him, or was it her? The door slowly opened and thank God it was her, a bit dishevelled with a bloody nose but I didn't care, it wasn't him and there was no gun. She told me not to panic, he had gone and not to worry about her as they were always fighting. She took me downstairs and I got dressed in double quick time. She told me that she had convinced her husband that nothing had been going on. I got the impression this wasn't the first time that this had happened. As I was leaving her house she whispered "call me tomorrow." "Of course I will" I replied. "No fuckin' way" I thought to myself. As I got to the end of the drive thinking I'd had a bloody close shave, I looked at my Corvette. A smashed window, the hood up and all the electrics ripped out. Methinks he did suspect after all…

I made it home after a five mile walk in a snow storm, a foot of snow and a temperature of minus five degrees but went to bed feeling a great sense of relief. Although I had never known that she was married, I made a solemn vow never to knowingly go with a married woman in the future. For the next couple of months, when collecting my luggage at Memphis airport after away games, there was a suspiciously high degree of damage to it.

I loved Memphis for many reasons. The people were absolutely fantastic. They were what I would call real Americans. When I talk to people in England and they say they've been to America, I ask them to which part? A lot of them say California, and I say they might as well have gone to Mexico. Others say Florida, and I say to them that they might as well have gone to Cuba!

You can't beat Southern hospitality. If you like music, well, even the dogs play guitar in Memphis. I was gutted to have to leave and so sad that time, distance and circumstances caused me to lose touch with some wonderful people.

I WAS TELT' THAT HE WAS GOOD AT THROWING THINGS AROUND!

104

41

GETTIN' HIGH LEGALLY

I'd always been fascinated by aeroplanes and flying in general, but had always been put off by the prohibitive cost of private lessons. My move to Memphis gave me the opportunity to satiate my desire for the 'high life'.

There was a flying school based at Memphis International Airport run by a guy called John who I had met one night in TGI Fridays. It so happened that he was a Rogues fan and after several bevvies he offered me an incredible deal for flying lessons in return for game tickets and several lines of coke, of which he was very fond!

A few days later I reported to the flying school for my first lesson where I was introduced to my instructor who was also a police pilot! My initial lessons were quite uneventful, an hour in the air alongside my instructor, then homework with my Jeppesen manuals. The routine changed however one Wednesday afternoon at the height of a red hot Memphis summers day. I had a fuckin' awful hangover after a particularly heavy night of drinking and I had actually thought about cancelling my lesson. I decided to go ahead with it as, if you cancelled on the same day, you got charged the full amount which, to me, was around $100 at the time.

We took to the air from Memphis International as usual then made our way over to Olive Grove, a small airstrip where we practised 'touch and goes' where you land and then take off again without stopping. We did about four and I was terrible, bouncing along the runway like a vintage plane in the movies. I wasn't surprised as I felt like shit! After the fifth attempt my instructor told me to pull off the runway and park beside the tiny control tower. I assumed he was going to ask me what was wrong and why was I flying so erratically, but I was wrong. He started getting out of the plane then casually turned around and said "Ok, go and do three by yourself"; he then proceeded to walk over to the tower to join the controller who was on duty, leaving me in a right state. "Oh well" I thought "in for a penny"…………

I sat and did a pre flight check list in the blazing heat that seemed to take forever and then made my way to the end of the runway. "Skipper 6757 Lima, ready for takeoff" I requested "Skipper 6757 Lima, clear for takeoff" replied the controller. I pushed forward on the throttle and, I've got to be honest, the take off is the easy bit; in fact you've got to fight to keep a light aircraft on the ground. Three quarters of the way down the runway the Beachcraft took to the air and that's when the situation suddenly hit home. I looked at the vacant seat next me where my instructor normally sat and I nearly shit meself. I had to land this bloody thing by myself. It's not like your first driving lesson where if you are struggling you can simply pull over. If you struggle in the air, you're fucked! I did my first circuit, landed and took off again perfectly, the tower told me I was clear for another go around which I commenced. As I was on the downwind leg I was supposed to lower the flaps to thirty degrees, which I forgot to do, this resulted in me being still at around one hundred feet in the air when I was above the beginning of the runway. "Skipper 6757 Lima, I think I better go around again" I stammered into the microphone. "I would if I were you son" replied the controller laughing hysterically.

I COULD'VE DONE A BIT OF DAMAGE IN THIS!

Well, I landed successfully for a third time and then picked up my instructor who shook me by the hand and congratulated me on going solo. We then made our way back to Memphis International and the flying school. When we entered the flying school's reception area, I was suddenly grabbed by the secretary, my instructor and John and was forced to the floor. They then proceeded to pull up my t-shirt and, with a pair of scissors, cut a half moon shape out of the bum end of it. They then let me up and my instructor signed and dated the piece of t-shirt with a black marker pen. I was completely bemused by the whole ritual until they explained that it was an initiation for pilots that had just gone solo. Seemingly it dated back to World War One when pilots dressed in shirts with shirt tails. They had only basic ground training before they were simply put into planes and sent to attack the enemy. Only a few ever returned and the ones that did had usually shit themselves! They then had to cut off the shitty shirt tails. This is where the tradition originated.

I continued to fly solo and I thought I was really gaining in confidence until the last time I took off from Memphis International Airport. I was well on my way to taking my 'flying test' and had only a solo cross country flight to do as well as clocking up a few more hours of flying time. I remember getting to the end of the taxi way with a long line of light aircraft behind me. I radioed in and told the controller that I was ready for takeoff. This deep southern drawl came back instructing me that Skipper 6757 Lima was clear for takeoff but to hurry, as there was an incoming DC 10. I looked up and could see the lights of the approaching plane. Now, in hindsight, I should have replied that I would wait and hold, however, with the long line of traffic behind me, I thought I'd hold everyone up so I taxied onto the runway and took off. Unfortunately, I hadn't realised that a rather large American Airline plane had just taken off on the same runway before me and so I hit a thing they call 'wake turbulence' which is twin vortices coming off the wings of a large plane that is flying low and slow. These two 'mini hurricanes' hit the Beachcraft and threw me to the other side of the airport. That is where I nearly shit me self again! The controller's calm voice came through the radio instructing me... "Skipper 6757 Lima, will you kindly resume your stated course".... "I would if I could"... I stammered and initiated an emergency go around procedure; well I think that's what it was called!

Fortunately for me, I landed safely and taxied back to the flying school, carefully checking my seat, t-shirt and shorts. I never flew again. That is why I am now a slightly nervous flyer knowing that, somewhere up in the sky, there's another inexperienced pilot, just like I was, ready to drop a right bollock!

42

MOVIN' ON UP...

All good things come to an end, so they say, and sure enough, the Memphis Rogues were sold to a gentleman called Nelson Skalbania who owned the Calgary American Football team and the Edmonton Oilers ice hockey team. The Rogues' players had to simply pack up all of their belongings, including their cars, and everything was picked up and shipped, lock stock and barrel up to Calgary Alberta!

As we'd never had a chance to sort out living accommodation, the players were put up in the Palliser Hotel in central Calgary, just opposite the train station. Our every need was catered for; all we had to do was sign for food, drink, room service and even the hookers who congregated on the hotel steps in the evening. The hotel even had a concert room where I saw Jack Jones about fifteen bloody times as he was performing a season there.

We had arrived in Calgary just before the start of the indoor season and the Memphis Rogues Booster Club, whose members were heartbroken at losing their soccer team, had arranged to fly up to Calgary to see the opening game.

A woman I knew called me and asked if she could stay with me when she came up with the Booster Club. I agreed because she was well fit and the women in Calgary were not; well at least the ones I had met.

Two days before the Booster Club arrived I'd received a parcel (yes, by Federal Express). I had picked it up from the hotel reception and, after signing for it, taken it up to my room. There was no information about the sender but it came from Memphis so naturally I opened it. Inside was a brand new hairdryer. Who the fuck would send me a hairdryer? And why? Anyhoo, nice gesture I thought, but why? Then I had a crazy thought, a thought daft enough to make me go and get a screwdriver and take the hairdryer to bits; when I eventually prized the hairdryer apart there it was, a package containing a quarter of an ounce of cocaine!

When the Booster Club eventually arrived and they had checked in to the hotel, my lady friend came to my room and immediately said she needed a shower after all the travelling. I was sitting having a bottle of Molson while watching TV when I heard her call out "Have you got a hairdryer Paul?" "No" I replied, "I just let my hair dry naturally." She didn't stay the night!

108

CALGARY BOOMERS 1980-81 INAUGURAL INDOOR SEASON

FRONT ROW: Terry Fisher (Assistant Coach), Dave Huson, Charlie Cooke (Captain) Rudi Schiffer (General Manager), Nelson Skalbania (Owner), Al Miller (Head Coach), Gerd Zimmermann, David Stride, Monty Jameson (Trainer)

MIDDLE ROW: Danny Andrews (Equipment Manager), Billy Gazonas, Farrukh Quraishi, Victor Kodelja, Danny Vaughn, Peter Stanley, Milan Stojsavljevic, Juan Carlos Molina, Dr. Geoffrey Haigh (Team Physician)

BACK ROW: Paul D'Agostino, Miguel Batalla, Carlos Salguero, John Houska, Tom Boric, Darryl Wallace, Steve Bradshaw, Paul Cannell, Jemal Serbo

THE CALGARY BOOMERS TEAM PHOTO. PROBABLY THE ONLY TIME I KNEW WHO WE HAD IN OUR TEAM!

I didn't like Calgary; in fact I fuckin' hated it! Apart from the fact that we were 'sold' there with no say in the matter, we were given no information at all about its climate. We moved there in the winter of 1981 and winter in Calgary is brutal. The average temperature in January is minus 11c. Although staying in the Palliser was more than comfortable, once out on the streets, the cold was incredible. I kept hearing on the local radio station phrases such as "The temperature today is going to reach a high of minus 20c, there is a ten percent chance of precipitation and we have a thirty second warning!" Now the first two parts of this I was familiar with; however the third part was new to me. After about three weeks I thought I'd ask a waitress in the hotel what this thirty second (it varied) warning was. "Simple" she replied. "If you leave your skin exposed for longer than thirty seconds, it'll fall off with frostbite" Nice to be telt!

The other thing that confused me (ok so I'm fuckin' easily confused) were the parking meters; there were electric plugs on them. Now I'd seen no electric cars or milk floats kickin' about so I never really thought to ask what they were for.

However I soon found out the reason for their existence after parking me Corvette, which had just come out of transit, at a meter. I'd only been for a couple of beers, jumped into the car, fired the beast up and the fuckin' engine exploded! I called out their version of the AA and when the patrol man eventually arrived, he lifted the bonnet, laughed out loud and explained to me that as the temperature was minus 22c, the oil and water had frozen solid in the engine. I should have plugged it into the electric socket on the parking meter to prevent this from happening. The cars in cold climates he said always had 'block heaters' fitted. A new engine was required for the vette and it cost over $2,000. Another reason to hate Calgary.

After a few games into the indoor season Ken Furphy, the manager of the Detroit Spinners oops I mean the Detroit Express (actually the Detroit Spinners might have been more appropriate) approached the Calgary management and inquired about signing me. I was pulled to one side, asked whether I was interested and within fifteen seconds I had left the Calgary Boomers. Yahoo!!!
Oh, and just to prove what a weird climate Calgary has; on the day I left for Detroit the temperature was 20c when the previous day it had been minus 10c. That is, as all good geography students will know, because of a wind called the Chinook.

43

TAKING IT ON THE CHIN...

I arrived in Detroit midway through the indoor season and although it wasn't as cold as Calgary, it was still no Memphis. I was curious as to what had made Detroit suddenly move in for me at that particular stage of the indoor season ... I was soon to find out.

The Washington Diplomats had been owned by the Madison Square Garden Company who had invested heavily into what they had thought would be the new cable television revolution. Their theory had been to buy a soccer franchise then set up a cable soccer network. However, after some years, the venture had stumbled and eventually failed. The company, headed by Sonny Werblin, had decided to fold the Diplomat franchise. Enter stage left, Jimmy "the chin" Hill. He recognised that Washington and neighbouring Virginia and Maryland had supported soccer in a big way, even though it hadn't been enough to justify the investment made by Madison Square Garden. The Diplomats had attracted crowds of around 30,000 and that was a damn sight more than the Detroit Express had been attracting to their expensive Pontiac Silverdome stadium. Hill owed millions of dollars in Detroit so an escape to Washington with its readymade support made sense. I was the final piece in the jigsaw, a hugely popular ex Diplomat returning home.

JIMMY HILL PONIFICATING ON THE TELLY... THE TWAT!

Things began brightly; the publicity machine went into full swing. P.M. Magazine, a national TV show, featured me on "24 Hours as the Mayor of Georgetown" in which a film crew followed me during a typical 24 hour day... this was long before the reality shows or spy-on-the-wall documentaries we take for granted today. Nike even made a special one off disco dancing shoe for me to wear on the show (great shoes but they didn't help my crap dancing!). I vividly remember being on the dance floor in Tramps nightclub in Georgetown, in the early hours of the morning, with Christian Barnard, the famous heart surgeon, Pele, Jimmy Hill and his son Duncan followed by a pissed film crew.

Organisation wise, things had come a long way in the last couple of years and the soccer players of the North American Soccer League had formed a players' union headed by John Kerr, an old team mate of mine from my loan spell with the Diplomats back in 1976. It had been funded by the American Football League Players Association, a union with huge funds that were 'keeping an eye' on this soccer revolution phenomena for obvious reasons. Because of my considerable experience, I was voted in as the Diplomats' player's representative. As their representative I had to communicate with the Yugoslavian, Hungarian, and Argentinean, Spanish, German, South African, French, Jamaican, Haitian members of the team as well as the obvious British, American and Canadian players. It was decided that I might as well be team captain at the same time. This was not a problem; I could get through to all of the players...... except the fuckin' Scottish!

Anyhoo, the season trundled along with average results but with good support. During the season we acquired the services of quite a well known player... Johann Cruyff! Imagine me, Johann Cruyff's captain! Although things seemed to be going pretty well with the crowds and results; rumours started circulating in the Diplomat office that there were financial problems.

Things came to a head one Thursday night in 'The Sign O' The Whale'. Me and Jimmy Steele, along with some of the front office staff were well tanked up in the early hours of the morning when Jamie Wheatley, the financial controller, dragged me to one side. "No Jamie" I said. "I'm taking Suzie home tonight"... "No, shut up you ass" was her reply, "I've got something to tell you, I shouldn't, but my conscience tells me I've got to". I almost sobered up. She continued, "If the team play on Saturday and anyone gets injured, none of the players will be covered by insurance. In fact, they haven't been covered for the last month. The club's insurance has been cancelled as we haven't been paying the insurance company". Then I did sober up!

"So anyone who gets injured is fucked?" was my take on it. "You put it your way" Jamie replied, "but for Christ's sake don't tell them I told you!". I left the Sign O' the Whale alone, to try and get my head around the situation.

Back home in Alexandria Virginia, I lay on the sofa watching "When the Boat Comes In" on PBS until 4am. What could I do without dropping Jamie in it? I had to do something. Apart from having players such as Johann Cruyff, we had players from English clubs such as Ross Jenkins and Trevor Hebbard... and one of their loan conditions was that they were adequately insured!

I went into training on the Friday, hung-over as usual but with an additional huge weight on my shoulders. I bumped into Jimmy Hill and Duncan Hill and asked them if everything was ok. "Everything's great" was their reply, "as long as we get a good result on Saturday." I had to bite my tongue; I didn't want to drop Jamie in it. During the training session I asked Ken Furphy, the manager, if there were any financial problems at the club. "Not that I know of" shrugged Furphy as he disappeared towards the locker room. I didn't know what to do.

After training I went in to see Jamie, explained my predicament and asked for some proof. She reached down and picked up what looked like a ream of A4 papers. "These are unpaid bills" she said, "they've paid nothing." I was flabbergasted. Jimmy Hill, the man who pontificates on TV about how to run a football club was a fraud!

Saturday... match day... versus the Toronto Blizzard. All the players were in the locker room at RFK Stadium, there were two hours until kick off. "Listen lads I need your attention, it's important" I called out, "there's something you need to know." These two simple phrases took about five minutes to be translated around all the nationalities in our team. "I've got to tell you that, if you play today and get injured, you are not covered by insurance." There was a general murmur as the Germans explained it to the Norwegians; the Yugoslavians explained it to the Hungarians, the Swedes to the Dutch and the South Africans to the Scots!

Just then Ken Furphy entered the locker room. "What's going on here?" inquired Furphy, "is this team bonding?" "No" I replied. "I want you to confirm that if the lads play today and get injured they ARE covered by insurance," "Of course they are" replied Furphy looking a little shaken. "Well that's not my information" I replied. "Go and get the money man and ask him because I'm not convinced."

"You're nothing but a trouble maker Cannell" replied Furphy. However, at that moment, Jimmy and Duncan Hill entered the locker room. "What's this all about?" asked the 'chinned one' sensing an atmosphere, "Cannell here, reckons that if the players get injured today, they're not covered by insurance"

Furphy replied. "Don't talk rubbish, of course they are" snapped Hill, but before he could go any further, I thrust a photocopy of the insurance cancellation notice in his face. "Oh well" he stammered, "What I meant was I would look after them if they get injured blah...blah...blah...blah...blah..." Some fuckin' chance!! Eight of us refused to play and were replaced by young American lads that didn't even know that they should have been insured in the first place! Then, within two weeks, the player's wages stopped and the club was placed in administration. What happened next was even more incredible.

As the player's representative, I was the focal point for all the players' questions. John Kerr, the head of the players union, could not get in touch with Jimmy or Duncan Hill. The administrators couldn't find them. None of the players were getting paid and the non US citizens didn't qualify, for some reason, for welfare benefits. They couldn't even afford to go home as the North American Soccer League had failed to secure from Jimmy Hill, the legal deposit of a players air fare home (a visa requirement I was led to believe) A warrant was put out for their arrest but still, after weeks, they could not be found. People were coming out of the woodwork from Detroit and all over the US trying to get their money back.

Then, mysteriously, Jamie Wheatley was informed that the Hills were leaving the US on a flight from Dulles airport. The tickets had been paid for and, as there was a warrant out for their arrest, the customs and tax people along with the police had been informed. The flight from Dulles was stopped on the runway and although the tickets had definitely been purchased, there was no sign of father or son.

The next day we were informed that Jimmy and Duncan Hill had flown out of National Airport (now named the Reagan Airport) to Toronto, which was classed as an internal flight and so no check had been made on them. Then, once they were in Canada where there was no warrant, they had fled back to England... owing businessmen and women, fans and players, millions of dollars. Did you ever wonder why Jimmy Hill never went to America during the World Cup which was held there???

What happened to the players? Well for the next two months I arranged illegal jobs for a lot of the players. Two Germans started working in a 'Bier Garden,' two South Africans in an Ethiopian restaurant, a Frenchman and an Argentinean as waiters in an Irish bar (don't ask!) and the Scots and English jobs behind the bars of DC's many British pubs........ Johann Cruyff had enough money to fly home!

44

IN THE BLUE RIDGE MOUNTAINS OF VIRGINIA

"Spread out in a bunch" barked Charlie Cooke the manager of the Memphis Rogues, "Spread out in a fucking bunch!"

The players in this practise match all looked bewildered; all except goalkeeper Bob Stetler... "He's always the same sometimes" he muttered to me.

Stetz was one of me best mates; when the Rogues wanted to sign me from the Washington Diplomats, I made it a condition that I would only sign if Stetler came too. Mind you, there was some professional logic in it because, he was a great goal keeper, American, and the Rogues needed an American keeper! We had decided to drive from D.C. to Memphis, me in my silver anniversary Corvette and him in his Datsun 280ZX. On Stetz' advice we both installed CB's, almost the height of technology at the time, in order to keep in touch and to avoid the cops.

BOB STETLER... AKA STETZ

115

FUCKIN' HELL IT'S PAUL CANNELL

The drive down was fantastic, the Blue Ridge Mountains of Virginia were awesome, nothing like I had expected them to be as I'd only ever heard of them on the Laurel and Hardy record. The trip passed without incident until I suddenly heard a crackling message over the CB... "Quaalude One to Coco Cannell over"... "Coco receiving go ahead"... "Quaalude One, beware brown bears"... "Coco Cannell, yup, keeping toot" I replied. Five minutes later a state trooper screeched in front of me, sirens and lights engaged, forcing me to pull over onto the hard shoulder. Stetz pulled in about one hundred yards in front of me. I'd never been in this situation before. A giant cop, who looked like an extra from the film Deliverance, with a gun in his hand leaned through my driver's side window and asked me for my licence, with the warning "Move very slowly!"

I did what I had done many times in the past and produced my English licence explaining that I was indeed English, moving from DC to Memphis, I played soccer and I loved Uncle Sam. This tactic was lost on Cletus Delroy Spuckler. "Rich little limey son of a bitch with a fast car, here's a ticket and an on the spot fine of $100". I had no idea of the law but fortunately I had the $100 bucks on me. I was just handing it over when Stetz walked up. "What's going on?" he said to Officer Cletus. The uniformed hillbilly replied "This limey dude was speeding so consequently I've given him a $100 on the spot fine, and thanks for stopping, you got one too!" Cletus returned to his patrol vehicle, $200 in his back pocket and drove off into the sunset. Stetz sat next to me, well pissed off about being $100 worse off. "Did you not hear me warning you about the Smokey bears?" he said. "Yes" I replied, "but I didn't know Smokey bears were called Cletus and drove fucking police cars!" The CB virgin had just lost his virginity!!!

STATE TROOPER CLETUS... OH FUCK!

45

ONE UP THE BUM, NO HARM DONE

Robert Alan Stetler was born in East Stroudsberg Pennsylvania. He had the looks of Robert Redford and, because of this, some people often made the mistake of thinking he was just a pretty face; which he was but he could fight; boy could he fight! He never actually intended to be a soccer player. He had been walking through Tampa University, where he had been involved in some sort of wrestling tournament when he had seen a crowd of people on the soccer fields of the campus. Being naturally curious, he wandered over. He asked what was going on and was told that the Tampa Bay Rowdies were holding tryouts for soccer goalkeepers. Stetz asked what a goalkeeper was and what he had to do and when told, he decided that he could 'catch a ball and stop it going in the net'. He joined the trials and ended up signing for the Tampa Bay Rowdies! That was in 1975… we were still teaching him the rules of soccer in 1980!

Stetz could always pull the lasses. One Saturday night after a Memphis Rogues game at the after game piss up, this gorgeous blonde approached us after we had both left the toilet. She had been to the game, loved soccer, loved Stetz and thought I was ok! She invited us back to her place for drink, drugs and sex. Not wanting to be 'party poopers' we agreed and made our way to the Germantown area of Memphis where we were ushered into a stylish townhouse. Nicola (we at least knew her name) poured some drinks and chopped up a dozen lines of coke on her glass coffee table. "Its good stuff" she informed us, "Pure Flake." She disappeared for some time then returned and said that she had prepared a bath, would we like to join her. Well, as Alan Freeman would say, "Not arf!"

Once naked in the huge whirlpool tub she asked us if we would shave her. Now getting rid of the five o'clock stubble in the morning with a hangover is hard enough, but shaving a woman's delicate bits when you're full of drink and toot is a bit dodgy. Anyway, she was depilated adequately and she then asked us both to 'make love' to her together; you know…two's up, just like in the porn films where they make it look so fuckin' easy, one potting the pink and the other potting the brown! However our performance fell short of any academy awards and it was, to say the least, rather clumsy.

Stetz was on top of her pounding away as I tried to thrust my engorged member, (as they say, in the porn magazines) into her at the same time…. "Argh, argh, argh"… I heard in my pissed state. "Eeee sorry pet" I apologised, "am I hurting you?" "No" replied Stetz, "but will you get your fuckin' cock out of my arse!"

Sadly, Stetz passed away in 1990.

ARL REET, IT'S NOT ME AND STETZ, BUT YOU GET THE IDEA, ME, HIM AND ONE LASS…

46

HIGH SPEED NEWS

On my return to the Washington Diplomats, I was approached by channel 9 to host a football segment every Friday evening on the six o'clock news. I had to go their studios in the afternoon and edit video footage of the teams playing over the weekend. I would then go home and write some notes in preparation for the live five minute spot on the sports segment of the news. This was a big deal for the Diplomats and the soccer community in general as it was the first time soccer had been recognised as a major sport on a major DC channel.

THE STUDIOS OF WTOP, HOME OF HIGH SPEED NEWS!

The first five or six weeks went great, the ratings were good, the station was happy, the Diplomats were happy, the soccer fans were happy, and I was very happy. On about the seventh week of the show Steeley, Stetz and I went on a right bender on the Thursday night, not getting in until daybreak. We went through the motions of training on the Friday morning then headed to the Sign O' the Whale for a much needed pick me up. After some lunch and a few pints Jimmy Finley, the bartender, reminded me that I should be heading up to Channel 9 to do the editing. I thanked him for reminding me and I decided it would be sensible to take a cab there, as I was way over the drink driving limit. Well, to be honest, it was really the bartender who took me car keys off uz and made me take a cab cos' I was still pissed…

I arrived at the station, edited some footage then took a cab back to the Whale. "How'd it go?" asked everyone, obviously expecting to hear that I had been thrown out. "Fine" I replied "no problems." It was about four o'clock and after making some notes on the back of some beer coasters, I decided I needed a couple of shooters to pick me up. Unfortunately Kamikazes, iced teas and a couple of Amoretto's didn't make me feel any better and I was in two minds whether to call the station and say I was sick. "Don't do that," Joe the local drug dealer interjected, "the show must go on" and he slipped me a gram of cocaine. I went to the office at the back of the pub (the men's toilet) and took my medicine. It made me feel much better. I went back to the bar, had another couple of pints then realised it was time to go to the studios. Just before I left to catch a cab, Finley called me over and put a green speckled tablet in my hand. "If you feel rough, take this pill" he said "we call them Christmas trees, the bartenders take them all the time to keep them buzzing on long shifts." I thanked him then took a mouthful of Steeley's beer and swallowed the pill.

I got to the station, did my spot, and then decided to take a cab straight home as I was feeling like shit. I felt a huge sense of relief that I had gotten through it all without letting anyone down.

When I got home, I put on the TV, lay on the couch and crashed out. I woke up at about 10.45pm and decided I needed a beer. The TV was still on channel 9 when the 11pm news came on. I watched it with little interest, a riot here, a murder there, a bent politician; you know, the usual stuff; until the sports segment came on. Now normally, my spot on the 6 o'clock news was live and it was never repeated on the later news…… until this week! I watched in total disbelief as I gabbled my way through the soccer feature sounding like a cross between the chipmunks and a 45rpm record being played at 78. You could see the two newscasters looking at each other and trying very hard not to laugh. I think the five minute spot took me all of two minutes to present. Now I knew why they had repeated the segment for the first time. It must surely have been shown on the U.S. version of 'It'll Be All Right on the Night'.

FUCKIN' HELL IT'S PAUL CANNELL

It took me a while to live this episode down, but thankfully, the Diplomats and the station saw the funny side of it and once I'd promised it would never happen again, nothing more was said by them............. which is more than I can say for the punters at the Sign O' the Whale!

47

LITTLE WET CORVETTE

My Corvette Stingray Silver Anniversary Edition was my pride and joy. Its purchase was my biggest extravagance in all my time in the States. It went like shit off a shovel, however the petrol gauge needle moved as quickly as the speedo' one!

I'd spent the previous evening at an all nighter in Crystal City, Alexandria and was making my way home in the Corvette at the start of the rush hour, about 7am. I had to cross a six lane highway in order to get to South Van Dorne Street where I lived. I noticed that there had been, or there still was, some road works going on as there were cones to the left of the highway then a gap, (which I presumed was to enable cars to cross to the other side), and then cones to the right. I hadn't noticed a large cement mixer trundling slowly down the road towards several workers taking a break. I waited for a gap in the traffic then made a bolt through the gap in the cones, to reach the other side of the road. As soon as I reached the middle of the highway my speed suddenly dropped and my car's wheels abruptly lost grip and started spinning wildly. In my hung-over state I couldn't understand what was happening. All I could feel was a sinking sensation, which is exactly what was happening, the car was sinking in the cement that the mixing truck had just laid! I tried to get out of the car but I couldn't open the door as the car had sunk in the newly laid cement up to the side window! I put my foot down on the accelerator, trying in vain to get some traction but the wheels just spun violently. Unfortunately the workers had seen what had happened and had run up to my car. The spinning wheels kicked up gallons of the wet cement absolutely covering the workers. They were not too amused. They plodged through the cement and dug around the drivers side door so I could open it and get out. I eventually reached the sanctuary of the embankment, up to my knees in wet cement and sat, dazed, alongside the workers. They explained that the gap in the cones was there to allow the truck to leave after laying the cement and that they should have replaced the cones immediately. Unfortunately they had been on a coffee break! The traffic was at a standstill in both directions with the rush hour motorists in stitches, laughing not only at the sinking Corvette but at the half a dozen road workers and myself covered in concrete sitting on the highway verge.

Suddenly, the sound of sirens filled the air and a couple of DC's finest weaved their way through the static traffic and pulled up alongside the vette which was now looking like a statue. The workers and I explained what had happened and the officers, trying hard not to laugh, said at least they had found the reason for the three mile tail back in both directions. The team leader of the road workers explained that it was a very special, quick drying cement and that it would probably cost $20,000 to relay the road. He also advised me that the Vette should be dragged out of the cement immediately.

TRY GETTING OUT OF THIS FUCKER WHEN THERE'S CEMENT UP TO THE WINDOWS!

A tow truck arrived several minutes later and dragged my car out of the quagmire. During this time I'd got on quite well with the cops as they had realised the situation was no fault of mine, even though, as one of them had noted, that I stunk of drink! He went on to say that my car needed to be steam cleaned immediately before the cement had set completely. He told me to follow him and that he'd take me to a commercial car cleaning company a couple of miles away. "Don't worry about speeding" he said "just follow me." We screeched off, him in front of me and his mate behind, with sirens blaring and lights flashing, doing 100mph down the highway pool lane. The cop car behind me had to drop back as there were chunks of concrete flying off in all directions. We arrived at the cleaners and they set about cleaning down the car as I chatted to the cops. "Well" said one of them. "Your Corvette has got to have one of the best under seals in the States!"

Needless to say I was late for training that day. I explained what had happened but Gordon Bradley the manager didn't believe me until I convinced him to take a ride in my car. There were still chunks of concrete, stuck around the exhaust pipes, which continued to fly off all over the place. Gordon apologized and laughed as he said it could only happen to me. There was still fuckin' shrapnel coming off two weeks later.

48

SHOCK JOCK

Howard Stern was probably the world's first 'shock jock,' a DJ who pushed what was allowed on the radio to the limit. As I was seen as a controversial player and he was a controversial DJ it almost made sense for the Washington Diplomats to get me on air with him. The programme they picked was called The Dating Game in which the celebrity had to interview three people (of the opposite sex I may add) and take the one selected out on a date, all broadcast live on DC 101 FM.

A YOUNG HOWARD STERN BEFORE HE RULED THE AIRWAVES

Terry Hanson, the public relations guy for the Diplomats, told me it would be a doddle. I'd end up going out on a date with a gorgeous bird and we'd be going to, wait for it, Barnum and Baileys 3 Ring Circus. Now the gorgeous bird bit seemed ok, but I was a bit apprehensive about the three ring circus bit! Never mind, I turned up at the DC 101 studio suitably tanked up, as it was only around the corner from the Sign O' the Whale. Obviously everyone in the bar was tuned into the station.

Howard Stern and his partner Robin Quivers made me more than welcome and helped me relax with a couple more drinks. They explained that there would be three women on the phone and that I had to ask them personal questions and from their answers, I would decide on the woman I'd take to the circus.

Once on air, all three women sounded great, I asked them their hobbies, what they did for a living, their star signs and other normal stuff ; then, during an ad break, Howard pulled me aside and said to me "Hey man, you've got a reputation for being a bad boy, why don't you shake it up a little, you know, ask the real questions, like say, have you got big tits, do you like it up the butt, do you swallow?" I got the message and once the break was over, I really got to know the three women! I decided on number two and arranged to meet her in the Sign O' the Whale the following night. Howard shook my hand and said it had been a tremendous show and they would follow up on the date. I however, was not convinced; I mean a voice on the end of the phone was one thing...

The next night I rang the Whale from Rumors (a bar close to the Whale) and spoke to Jimmy Finley the usual bartender. "Jimmy" I said, "is there a bird in there looking for me?" "Hell yes" he replied. "There was a hell of a fat bird who said she liked it up the arse, but she left about ten minutes ago with John the window cleaner who's just inherited that money"... I didn't go to the circus!

Howard Stern went on to sign a $400 million deal with Sirius XM which will keep him shocking listeners until 2015.

49

I'M COMIN' HOME NEWCASTLE

When Jimmy and Duncan Hill's Washington Diplomats went bankrupt, the player's wages obviously ceased being paid. The administrators had already been called in and had set about realising the company's assets; of course there were none, except for the players. The players association, our union, informed us that the whole team were up for sale but it could take months before fees and salaries could be negotiated.

Time dragged on and eventually I had to put the two condominiums I had bought as an investment up for sale through a friend of mine, who worked for Century 21 real estate. He warned me however, that my timing was crap to say the least as, at the time, interest rates were at an all time high and American mortgages, unlike the British, were all fixed rate. Indeed, that is why the De Lorean car company had failed as car loans were prohibitively expensive and John De Lorean the founder of the company had tried to raise money through a huge drug deal. I hung around for a few months but nothing seemed to be happening so I decided to come back to England until there was some news on the transfer or house sale front. I didn't know what to do about my Corvette, I still owed cash on it and again, it was a terrible time to try to sell it. As it was insured, I decided to leave it in the Giant Supermarket car park opposite my condo in Alexandria. Someone was bound to steal it whilst I was in England. I booked my airline tickets, had couple of nights getting off me face, then headed back to Newcastle.

It was great to get back home to the Toon even though the reason behind it was pretty shit. I was stayin' at me mam and dads house in High Heaton, just up the road from the Corner House, the pub that had always been my local. Nothing had changed in the nine months I had been away, none of the regulars had died and they were all in their usual positions in the bar. I'd been home for about three weeks and had still heard nowt' from the States. I was having me usual lunchtime couple of pints in the Corner when in walked a couple of people I hadn't seen for years, Geoff Allen and Stuart Boam, two ex Toon players.

"Bloody hell" exclaimed Allen, "what are you doing in here? I thought you were in America". I explained what had happened and that I was in Newcastle until things had been sorted out. "What are you two doing these days?" I asked them. They explained that they were managing Mansfield Town, a team in the English fourth division, and that they had come up to Newcastle to watch a player they were interested in.

After several pints, Stuart asked me how I was keeping fit. "Well, I walk down here" I replied, laughing. "Why don't you come down to Mansfield for a while?" chirped in Geoff. "It'll keep you fit and you can help us with the younger players. We'll put you up in a hotel and pay all your living expenses as well as a little backhander." Now this seemed like a good idea. I was getting a bit bored, I did need to keep fit and I got on really well with both of them. It seemed a 'win win' situation, well at least it did to a thick Geordie like me!

I travelled down to Mansfield and true to their word the hotel (a decent one) was booked and all I had to do was sign for everything. The training was hard but good fun and I spent quite a bit of time coaching their youth squad. After training, everyone usually made their way to the Portland, a pub just down the road from Field Mill, Mansfield's home ground which was run by a former Stags player called Sandy. One day, after a few pints, I made my way back to me hotel where I received a phone call from Geoff Allen. He invited me for an Indian meal with himself and Stuart Boam just to "have a natter." The restaurant was in the centre of Mansfield and was a favourite with the players. The meal was quite uneventful, the food was decent and the alcohol plentiful. Suddenly, out the corner of my eye, I saw movement at the base of a decorative curtain. "Hey" I burst out "'I've just seen a bloody rat!" "Don't be daft; it's the drink" replied Geoff "no honestly, I did!" I insisted, and pointed to a tail sticking out from under the curtain. They believed me then. Stuart shouted for a waiter and pointed out the rat to him. The waiter got the manager who said he thought that we were joking and he felt it was a joke that was in bad taste. As we were explaining that we were deadly serious, the waiter went over to the curtain and shook it. The rat scurried off through the waiters legs, towards the manager who kicked it and it flew into the air. The dazed rat landed by the kitchen door. The manager casually walked over to the rodent, picked it up by the tail and disappeared through the kitchen door, never to be seen again.

We looked at each other in total disbelief then quietly got back to drinking our vino. Geoff broke the silence by asking me if I was enjoying training with them. I replied that I was. "Well" he continued "as you've heard nothing from the States, why don't you play a few games for us?" "I can't" I replied, "The administrators hold my international registration." "Don't worry; I'll sort that out" said Stuart, "I'll see you after training tomorrow."

THE FOOTBALL ASSOCIATION

LIMITED

Patron: HER MAJESTY THE QUEEN
President: H.R.H. THE DUKE OF KENT
Chairman: SIR HAROLD THOMPSON, C.B.E., F.R.S.

Secretary:
E. A. CROKER

Telegraphic Address:
FOOTBALL ASSOCIATION, LONDON, W2 3LW

16 LANCASTER GATE, LONDON, W2 3LW

Ref: JAY/

16th December, 1981.

P.Cannell Esq.

Dear Sir,

re: International Clearance Certificate.

Further to my letter of ---------------- I have to inform you that you have been granted a Clearance to play in England by the United States Soccer Federation*

You are now free to sign for any affiliated Club in this country.

Yours faithfully,

Ealoroker

Secretary.

* This Clearance is conditional subject to final clearance being granted following decision of U.S. Bankruptcy Court in respect of Washington Diplomats S.C.

MY INTERNATIONAL CLEARANCE SUDDENLY APPEARED FROM OUT OF NOWHERE!

The following day, I knocked on the gaffer's door, entered and sat down opposite him and Geoff. Stuart thrust a typed piece of paper in front of me and said "just sign that and you'll be able to play for us until you get back to the States." Like a mug, I signed the paper, in duplicate and thought no more about it as I was in a hurry to get to the Portland.

I played around six games for the Stags and thoroughly enjoyed it, the lads were great, the supporters were great and the town was full of the Geordies who had moved down to the Nottinghamshire coal fields when the pits in the north east had closed down. However I still knew there were unresolved issues in the States and so I went to see Stuart and Geoff to tell them I had to return. "You can't do that" they said in almost unison. "We've bought you!" It transpired that they had in fact bought me off the administrators in Washington and that the piece of paper I had signed, but never read, was indeed a two year contract! I was not a happy chappy, however the two of them charmed their way out of it explaining it was in my and the club's best interests.

I played until the end of the season then headed back to D.C. to sort out me affairs. I got back to my condo (which was still unsold) then walked over the road to the Giant Supermarket car park. To my dismay my Corvette was still there, totally intact apart from a bloody flat tyre. What happened to all the decent car thieves? The real estate agent told me that he had received offers on my two condos but for $30,000 less than I had paid for them. I told him he may as well accept the offers as I couldn't afford to keep paying the mortgages on them and it would be only a matter of time before the bank foreclosed. I must hold the fuckin' record for being the only person ever to lose money on property in Washington DC! I left my Corvette in a parking lot next to the Sign O' The Whale never to be seen again. I then found out that the $80,000 Jimmy Hill owed me for an unpaid signing on fee and back wages was simply part of the rumoured $2 million he owed creditors. So much for the twat pontificating on television on how people should run football clubs. He even scammed Coventry City, where he had been the chairman, by buying players at reduced rates and 'transporting' them to America where they were re-valued! A con man, no more, no less! After a couple of weeks catching up with old mates and of course getting drunk, I realised I had to head back to Mansfield to resume my career. I must admit I was pretty pissed off having to leave the States.

Once back in Mansfield the gaffer told me he had found a nice house in the Rainworth area of the town, far better than living in a hotel. The season started badly and pretty soon Stuart and Geoff were under pressure from directors and supporters to improve results. One of the Mansfield players was a fellow

FUCKIN' HELL IT'S PAUL CANNELL

Geordie called Ray Blackhall, who had been at the Toon around the same time as me. I remember him asking me over a pint whether I, like him, had ever been scared to take a throw in at St James' Park. It transpired that a couple of times, when the ball had gone into the crowd in the paddock area of the ground, when he had gone to retrieve it, he got a load of stick. "It was bad enough getting stick off the supporters" he said "but getting stick off the peanut seller as well!"

Needless to say after a few more poor results, Stuart and Geoff were sacked and Ian Grieves took over as manager. I was totally pissed off now. My two mates, who had conned me into signing for Mansfield, but who had at least made it a pleasant experience, were gone, and in came a totally new face.

Ian was a decent manager with a lot of experience but it just wasn't the same. After a few games under his new regime, we were playing Crewe Alexandra and we were losing 1-0 in freezing snowy conditions at half time. Once we got into the warmth of the dressing room, I decided to put a vest on underneath my yellow Stags top. "You are not fuckin' enjoying this are you?" I said to myself, my thoughts drifting to the sun kissed beaches of Clearwater and the night life of Memphis and DC. At the end of the second half, as we left the pitch, I said to the boss, "I won't be back on Monday, I quit". "You can't" replied Grieves, "you've got a year left on your contract." "Just rip it up!" I replied and, after getting changed, I drove home to Newcastle. That was it. The end of my professional football career...

50

DIVVEN'T ASK ME

As I've said, The Corner House in Heaton had been my local pub for decades but since I was now living in North Shields, I hadn't been in for quite a while. I'd been to see me mother, who was getting' on a bit, who lived on Holystone Crescent, just up the road from the pub and so, on my way home, I thought I'd pop into the Corner for a pint. It was quiz night and the place was packed. I recognised some of the locals and we ended up having a natter and several more pints, just as one does. "Paul" shouted some lads that I knew at one table. "It's the sports round, howay man, giz a hand." Well not wanting to appear thick I said "Aye, but just the sports round cos I've got to get back." We got up to question number eight and, quite honestly, so far I hadn't been much help. Question number eight was "Who was the last player to score a goal both home and away in a Tyne/Wear derby in the same season?" "Gary Rowell" I piped up with an air of supreme confidence. "Are you sure it was Gary Rowell?" asked the team captain. "Yes" I replied, "I'm positive!" The team were playing their joker on the sports round to double the points they scored so it was important to get it right.

THE CORNER HOUSE, HEATON. MY SPIRITUAL HOME

The sheets were handed in, marked by the quizmaster and the answers read out. Question eight; the answer wasn't Gary Rowell, the answer was fuckin' Paul Cannell. Oh well… time to go!

P.S.… I believe that since then, the one and only Shola Amoeba (oh sorry, that's a unicellular organism) I mean, Shola Ameobi has taken the record off me.

51

THE TIMES THEY ARE A CHANGING

I've lost count of the amount of times people have asked me if I'm pissed off with all the money footballers are getting these days. They're usually surprised when I tell them that I'm not envious at all. There simply wasn't the money in the game in the seventies and eighties to pay the players that kind of money. They're also under the misapprehension that the directors of Newcastle were on the fiddle. The likes of Lord Westwood who ran a toy company, Gordon McKeag who was a solicitor, Stan Seymour who ran a sports shop, Squadron Leader Jimmy Rush who owned a glassware company; Doctor Rutherford was a surgeon and Fenton Braithwaite, a plastic surgeon et al were put in the same bracket as the Great Train Robbers by the supporters. Unfortunately in my opinion they were wrong. The only money coming into the club was through the turnstiles and the cost of admission was very low. The directors got their jollies from the champagne, fine wine and first class travel at home and abroad. They were professionals in their own right, doctors, business men and legal eagles. The running of a football club was a part time occupation.

Mind you, I do remember, in St James' Park there was a room alongside the dressing room that contained what could be loosely called a computer. It counted the number of clicks on each turnstile (one click, one spectator) around the ground and it was monitored by a member of the 'on duty' fire brigade. I remember that when I looked at the crowd numbers on the machine there was always one turnstile that was mysteriously 'offline.' The other problem was that there was no way the on duty fire officer could accurately tell how many spectators were in each sector of the ground because most of the turnstile operators allowed two people to squash through at the same time and got a back hander from the extra punter. No wonder the job of a turnstile operator was handed down from father to son. A nice little earner!

The reason players wages escalated was twofold, technology and the Bosman ruling. From August 1964 the BBC screened Match of the Day on Saturday evenings. As it was on the BBC, no advertising was allowed on the player's shirts; even the logo of the shirts manufacturer had to be covered up. So, assuming your game wasn't on Match of the Day, the only people that saw any advertising were the home supporters who saw the same adverts week in week out. This obviously didn't appeal to the advertising agencies who wanted national coverage.

One of the daft conditions imposed on the B.B.C by the Football League was that the game due to be shown on Match of The Day that Saturday, had to be kept secret so that it wouldn't affect the home gate. This was pretty stupid as, with the old fashioned technology, the B.B.C. had to start setting up its equipment on the Monday before the Saturday match........hardly a secret!

The only other game that was screened was on a Sunday afternoon. An I.T.V. programme called 'Shoot.' It had various presenters including 'Geordie' George Taylor, and the ex B.B.C presenter Kenneth Wolstenholme, famed for the "They think it's all over... it is now!" World Cup Final phrase. During one of my first games that was shown on Shoot, a ball was played up to me and Wolstenholme announced "It's a through ball to Cannell who turns and shoots... oooah! Doesn't he look like Kenny Ball without his Jazzmen?" Shoot had a limited local audience on Tyne Tees Television. So, although advertising was allowed, it didn't appeal to the ad agencies. However, as technology advanced, it took less time and less equipment to show games live or recorded. Every team's games were broadcast in some way, even those in the fourth division. Then with the birth of the Premier League and the deal with BskyB, the number of viewers skyrocketed.

KENNETH WOLSTENHOLME
"THEY THOUGHT IT WAS ALL OVER"

It was brilliant news for the ad agencies as the games were not only beamed nationally but internationally and it was very easy to target the adverts. Not only did the clubs get money from stadium advertising but from shirt sponsorship and from Sky. The clubs were awash with money, but it wasn't going to the players, it was going to the clubs; All that was about to change with the Bosman Ruling. On the 15th of December 1995 the Bosman ruling was passed which enabled the players to move to another club when their contract ran out. Previously, when a player's contract expired, his club could still demand a transfer fee for the player, and if they didn't get the money they wanted, the player was stuck in limbo as the players club still held his registration. Now, after Bosman, the players held the power. It meant, at the end of their contract, the player could move to another club free and the money that the club would have paid to sign the player could in fact go to the player via a signing on fee and higher wages. This prompted clubs to sign players for longer terms of contract, sometimes up to ten years and not the one, two or three which had previously been the norm.

I'm all in favour of the players getting decent money; after all, it's the players who put the bums on seats in stadiums and in front of the TV screens, not the directors. Let's face it, if a crap player demands 50k a week, he won't get it. By in large, players get what they are worth. Don't be fooled by the wages you read about in the papers. If you read that a player has been signed for £30 million and is on £100k a week, don't take it as gospel. The team that has sold him will confirm the figures because it makes them look like they've got a great price for possibly a fan favourite (and they've cut their wages bill), the team that have bought him will agree with the figures because it makes them look they're paying big money to get the best players. The player won't deny it because it makes other clubs think he's worth the transfer fee and his salary, and his agent definitely won't deny it because it makes him look like a great agent that other players will want to use! It's a win, win, win, win scenario, but hey, it's often not true!

No I don't resent the money the players get now, they're in the entertainment business, no different from actors such as Tom Cruise or singers like Tom Jones or Neil Diamond. In fact, I liken football teams to West End musical casts; for example, Les Miserables and Man United. They play in the best stadia and the best theatres, they have the best cast and the best teams, they pay the most money to get the best talent and it doesn't matter whether you go on a Saturday night or to a Wednesday matinee, they'll give you a great show and always give one hundred percent.

The only thing I think should change in football is that more of the players salary should be performance related, no win, less money. The one thing I hate is when a player appears quite happy to sit on the bench still pocketing his wages. Never forget to bear in mind that the majority of football players are not on massive salaries; in a profession that can be cut short in a split second. Soccer is going the same way as American football, eventually the spectators will hardly contribute to the finances of the club. In fact, the club may make more money if they were playing in an empty stadium with no overheads. God, I hope that's not a fuckin' premonition!

52

WHAT A DIFFERENCE A DECADE MAKES

Do I like the present day game? Yes, but not as much as I did before technology took over the sport. What do I mean by technology you may ask; well mostly the changes to the football, the pitches, our overwhelming health and safety rules and slow motion action replays.

In the late 80's and early 90's, football or soccer was almost a global sport. It was played professionally in just about every country in the world and it was the number one spectator and participation sport. Only one nation was missing, the one nation that would make football truly global and that was the United States of America.

Professional leagues had come and gone in the States, the two latest being the A.S.L (American Soccer League) and the N.A.S.L (North American Soccer League) which folded in 1984. F.I.F.A. were desperate to get the US back into the fold as, with the US on board, they could get their greedy grubby paws into more advertising revenue (hmmm, and you thought it would be for a football reason...).

They had a cunning plan (yes Baldrick could have been on the FIFA board). Let us stage the World Cup in a nation with no professional soccer league and where the citizens have voted with their feet that they don't want soccer! Does that sound a bit like Qatar? Anyhoo, FIFA in all their collective wisdom, voted to stage the World Cup in the U.S! They had market researchers interviewing people at sporting events and in bars all over America to try to discover why soccer was not a popular spectator sport, even though it was the country's biggest participation sport by a mile. The answer came back and, unequivocally the reason was lack of 'points.' The Americans were used to big scores... basket ball 89-90, American football 18-12 and baseball 5-8, were all typical scores. Now, to an American, a soccer match, no matter how technically brilliant that after 90 minutes ends up 1-0 is boring. They simply didn't appreciate the 'beautiful' game. So F.I.F.A. set about rectifying this with 'test matches' around the States.

They played with a 30 yard offside line, no offside, wider goals, higher goals, wider AND higher goals but none of these increased the goals scored significantly (obviously, altering the size of the goals was done within sensible limits). They then had a brainwave, or at least Adidas did. They decided that if they could alter the path and speed of the ball in the air, it would make it more difficult for goalkeepers. Now remember that Adidas is the sole sporting goods manufacturer of the World Cup. Adidas and F.I.F.A. have an almost insidious relationship. In other words, it stinks!

From out of nowhere, Craig Johnson, an Australian who had played for Middlesbrough and Liverpool, invented the rubber finned football boot that became known as the 'Predator'. The idea was that the rubber fins on the boot would increase the friction on the ball so that more spin or bend could be produced. The continentals and the South Americans had always been able to score more spectacular goals than the British. This was because they played in a hotter and sometimes more rarefied atmosphere and they played with a ball that was lighter and made up of pentagonal panels. The ball was rough on the outside caused by dry, dusty pitches, which gave more grip on the ball, enabling the player to impart more spin. People wonder why the players in England during the 70's and 80's could never score goals like they do now. The reason is simple. We played with a rock hard, shiny Mitre Multiplex football, one up from a T ball, which was usually wet. If, when taking a free kick, you hit the ball over the defensive wall, it usually went over the stand! Remember Peter Lorimer, the free kick expert for Leeds United? Well even he had to have a 20 yard run up to get enough power to beat the keeper.

What a coincidence, the first Predator football boot appeared in 1994, the same year as the World Cup was held in America!

The fins, in my opinion were a gimmick. The real changes came in the construction of the football. Instead of having a conventional bladder, balls were constructed with up to three or four baffles (sections) which separated the pressurised air inside the ball. When a player kicked the ball, the closest baffle to be struck would be compressed so that the air pressure would be raised causing the football to swerve. A bit like having a weight put on part of the ball. The surface of the ball was also changed. Gone was the flat shiny surface and in came a dimpled one, just like a golf ball, which again increased the ability of the ball to swerve and travel through the air quicker than before. The balls were tested in wind tunnels to measure the degree of movement in flight. The end result was that the goals scored increased. I'd like to say very clever, well done Adidas, but I can't because I think these alterations have spoilt the game for several reasons.

At one time the British had the best goalkeepers in the world. We used to laugh at our continental counterparts who flapped at crosses and punched and patted the ball away. Now we realise why the continentals couldn't catch the ball like the British keepers could. They were playing with balls that were unpredictable.

THE ORIGINAL PREDATOR FOOTBALL BOOT

Of course other football manufacturers had to keep up with Adidas and went to even greater lengths to make the ball deviate through the air. Players then realised it was more advantageous to 'fall down' or take a 'dive' anywhere within thirty yards of the opposition goal as you had a greater chance of scoring a goal from a dead ball situation than in open play. This created major problems for officials, did the player take a dive and deserve a yellow card, or was he fouled and the defender given a yellow card or even sent off? Throw ins became like corner kicks and goalkeepers kicked the ball off the ground as it travelled further than when kicked out their hands. Keepers had another problem. Previously, in order for a wide player to cross the ball from the bye line, he had to arc the ball in order to reach the central goal area; the keeper had time to judge the balls trajectory and collect the cross. The new ball could be clipped in flat, preventing the keeper from coming for the ball or if he did, risk being stranded in no man's land. I don't know why they didn't go the full fuckin' distance and blindfold the goalkeeper! Oh, they couldn't because of health and safety!

The pitches have also spoilt the game. Ok, in theory, everyone likes to play on perfectly groomed surfaces but after a while the spectators get bored with the twenty seven passes from back to front that eventually ends up with the keeper kicking the ball up the field. Where have all the snow covered, ankle deep in mud, dusty, rock hard pitches that made the British footballer the most adaptable in the world gone? If a pitch gets a bit of mud on it these days, they sue the PLC that laid the pitch, and then get it re-laid by another fuckin' one.

Action replays are great for the televised game but crap for the officials. They don't have the benefit of them and quite rightly so. I wouldn't ban action replays but I would ban slow motion replays. The reason… every tackle in slow motion looks evil, it makes tackles look late and high, and every aerial challenge gives the impression that the players have used their elbows. When the same incident is shown from different angles, it complicates the issue rather than clarifying it. Real time replays yes, slow motion replays NO!

Finally, health and safety, the laws that say when it snows the game gets called off; not because it would spoil the game or cause a danger to the players, but because a spectator might slip! The fans of the 60's, 70's and even the 80's must be crying into their pints, well….. That's if the food hygiene people would allow it…

53

WICKED-PEDIA

When you see your kids doing their homework and they go to Wikipedia for references, tell them to be careful...

I, like many others, typed my name into Wikipedia, just to see if anything appeared. I was honestly fuckin' amazed that anything at all came up as I'd never realised that just about everyone and everything on this planet is on Wikipedia. The first bit of information about me seemed fairly accurate but so it should be, as I was told that anyone who put stuff on the site had to have some sort of specific knowledge i.e. journalists, historians or at least people who have never been sectioned! It gave the dates I played for teams, appearances, goals scored and the like. However what came up after that was totally bizarre. It read.....

"He is currently making a successful career in semi professional disco dancing, as well as regularly being ranked in the top 3 in Europe at naked pot holing, which he has sadly had to give up, due to his previous commitments as a human guinea pig at Beamish Museum where he met his current partner Trevor. Amongst other interests is playing bandits, walking poodles, drinking cider and horsing a female Frank Spencer lookalike."

Paul Cannell

From Wikipedia, the free encyclopedia
(Redirected from Paul cannell)

Paul Cannell (Born Newcastle upon Tyne 2 September 1953) is a footballer who played forward for Newcastle United between 1972 - 1978. He made 62 appearances and scored 18 goals, before moving to the United States. Cannell was the substitute for the 1976 League Cup Final, which Newcastle lost 2 - 1 to Manchester City.

In his career as a whole, he played for Newcastle United, two spells with the Washington Diplomats (1978-79 80 Apps 37 Goals, 1981 13 apps 1 goal) 1 , the Memphis Rogues (27 Apps 8 Goals), Calgary Boomers, the Detroit Express, North Shields, and Mansfield Town.

He is currently making a successful career in semi professional disco dancing, as well as regularly being ranked in the top 3 in Europe at naked pot holing, which he has sadly had to give up, due to his previous commitments as a human guinea pig at Beamish Museum where he met his current partner Trevor. Amongst other interests is playing bandits, walking poodles, drinking cider, and horsing a female Frank Spencer lookalike.

Resources

A Complete Who's Who of Newcastle United, by Paul Joannou

Retrieved from "http://en.wikipedia.org/wiki/Paul_Cannell"
Categories: 1953 births | Living people | English footballers | NASL players | Washington Diplomats (NASL) players | Memphis Rogues players | Detroit Express players | Calgary Boomers players | English football biography stubs

- This page was last modified on 10 March 2008, at 18:50.
- All text is available under the terms of the GNU Free Documentation License. (See **Copyrights** for details.)
  Wikipedia® is a registered trademark of the Wikimedia Foundation, Inc., a U.S. registered 501 (c)(3) tax-deductible nonprofit charity.

I SUPPOSE IT DID MAKE IZ INTERESTING !!!!!

54

ME LIFE BEHIND BARS

I'd never prepared for life after football. It had never crossed my mind that I would have to earn a living in the real world; I'd also be starting from scratch as I'd lost all me money in America! Once I got back to Newcastle I set about finding a job. What did I know as much about as I did football? Drinking!

I started working for Vaux breweries, a Sunderland based firm. I assume I was employed because they thought that as an ex-Newcastle player, I would have a better chance of getting their products into the pubs and clubs north of the river Wear. During my time at Vaux I had to deal with people who needed finance in order to initiate or complete leisure industry projects. It also meant that I found out which pubs and clubs were in financial trouble. One such business was a private members club on Newcastle Quayside called The Press Club. They owed Vaux around £30,000 and were struggling to keep up the loan repayments. I got in touch with a friend of mine, Peter Bell, who was always looking to make a quick buck and explained the situation to him. We decided to go into partnership; I got Vaux to lend Peter thirty grand, he bought the club off the grateful owners and lo and behold, we had the Press Club! As the name suggests, it was a private members club for members of the press. Colin Milburn, the ex England cricketer now a sports reporter, was a regular visitor, along with other well known established sports hacks from the daily tabloids. They had it sussed … they didn't fight against each other trying to get scoops, they would sit around the club having a few pints and took it in turn to have the story of the day. I presume the job was easier in those days as the players and the reporters got on well together; they socialised together and actually trusted one another. Other regulars included members of Tyne Tees Television, the B.B.C. and, for some reason the fire brigade. Things were going really well until Vaux caught wind of my involvement in the club and so I had to break up the partnership and go back to my proper job as a free trade rep.

The trouble was there were always deals to be done out there, that's what I was getting paid for. It was just that I wasn't supposed to be getting involved in the deals. At this time, Vaux were in possession of a property on Waterloo Street, Newcastle, called Dingwalls which was lying empty. They had it on the market for a quarter of a million quid but there had been very little interest. I decided to take a look at the books and discovered that it was costing Vaux five hundred pounds a week for this place to lie empty. This was because they had lent Harvey Goldsmith, the concert promoter, a load of cash to set up these Dingwalls around the country but they had gone bust. Vaux had taken the buildings lease as security against the loan and so when he defaulted, they grabbed it. What they hadn't realised was that once they took possession of the lease, they were responsible for paying the rent to the landlord (Star Cinemas) and that rent was five hundred quid a week!

At the time I was friends with a bloke called Dave Christie who was the boss and lead singer of a band called Zoots Navarro who were huge, at the time, on the social club scene. Dave or "Zoot" had always said that he would love to have his own club and so when I told him about Dingwalls, he was all ears. I suggested that I would say to Vaux that he was interested in the property but there was no way he was going to pay two hundred and fifty grand for it. He was, I would tell them, willing to take the club off their hands and pay the legal fees but that was it, as the property was in need of substantial renovation. I put the idea to the financial controller at Vaux, he put it to the members of the board and the deal was done. Zoot and I were over the moon; however we were not joking when we had said the place needed a lot of work done to it, especially to turn it into a cabaret style venue. In fact, it required two hundred thousand pounds worth of renovation and Zoot and I hadn't got a bean! Not a problem. I approached Dryboroughs, a brewery I knew were keen to establish themselves in the North East and spoke to their rep. a real character called Ronnie Cheatham. Ronnie had been in the beer trade for years and what he didn't know wasn't worth knowing. He wasn't interested in how the deal was done as long as it produced the beer sales to stack up against the loan. I told a little lie... that the renovations and alterations would cost £400,000, we had £200,000 and we needed Dryboroughs to put up the other £200,000. Ronnie approached his directors with the deal and they approved it with one condition; that we put up the first two hundred thousand quid. I was expecting this however, and I'd already had a word with my building contractors in Gosforth. They would start work on the club, that we were going to call Zoots, and half way through the job they would give us a receipt which showed that Zoot and I had paid £200,000. Once we had that we would give the receipt to Dryboroughs who would then release their £200,000 ... the actual cost of the project. The plan actually worked!

At the time I was engaged to a girl I had met at school called Julie Barker. She'd stuck by me all the time I'd played in the States and then Mansfield and now I was back in Newcastle our friends and families assumed that we would tie the knot. It was "knot to be". A few days before the club was due to open, I met a good looking female rep. who had called in to sell us some advertising space in the now defunct Herald and Post newspaper. To cut a long story short, we hit it off; I left Julie and ended up marrying Linda Huntington. I can't say we had everyone's blessing however; in fact we ended up getting married in London so that when asked "Does anyone object ?" we wouldn't have masses shouting out "We do".

I ran the club with Dave for just under a year during which time I left Vaux Breweries (well I thought I'd better) however we started to have arguments over which creative direction the club should take and, as the club was called Zoots, I decided to sell my share of the business to Zoot! We split on good terms and Zoots continued to do well until the band Zoots Navarro split up. Once again I was out of work but this time out of choice. I decided to start publishing hotel magazines. I had seen them during my time in America; they were placed in each hotel bedroom and at reception and they gave the hotel guests information about local amenities, things to do and things to see. They were financed by advertising. I set up an office in Jesmond, Newcastle, above the offices where my new wife Linda worked, also selling advertising. One lunchtime, I got a phone call from a friend of mine who told me he had some knocked off microwaves for sale. I telt' Linda that I was popping out for a while then set off, in me motor, to his house which was just off Chilly Road in Heaton. When I got there I discovered that the microwaves weren't "knocked off" they were simply from Makro, they just seemed cheap. When he realised that I wasn't interested in the ovens, he changed the subject and said that he'd just got some new cocaine from a friend of his, would I like to try some? Of course I said yes, thanked him, then left and drove back to Jesmond. I was just about to get out of my car when four other motors screeched to a halt, surrounding me. It was like something from Miami Vice. A plain clothed cop ordered me out of my car and demanded I empty my pockets. I suddenly realised that I was not only handing him a packet of tabs, my office keys and a dirty snot rag but also a wrap of cocaine. He asked me what the packet contained and I replied, in all honesty, that I was told it was cocaine (a dumb answer I was to find out later). I was arrested, taken to Gosforth cop shop and questioned, for what seemed like hours. When I explained that I would have to tell me missus what was going on, they decided to drag her out of her place of work (which went down really well!) and took her to our flat to search for more drugs, which of course they didn't find. During my questioning, it became apparent that I had been arrested, not by the normal police, but by the drug squad and that they knew who I was and that I'd played for the Toon. Without saying it directly, he explained that they knew I'd been in the wrong place at the wrong time. They were going to send the confiscated substance away to be analysed but I shouldn't worry as I would probably hear no more about it. I felt a lot better on hearing those words.

After my release, a couple of days passed uneventfully until the Wednesday, I believe, when we stopped for petrol on our way to Linda's parent's house. After filling up I went into the shop to pay. On the counter, next to the till, was a pile of early edition Evening Chronicles with a front page headline which read "COCAINE CANNELL." I panicked and thought about buying the entire pile until I realised that it would be a futile exercise. I bought a couple of copies (with my head down) and got back into the car. I asked Linda if her parents got the Evening Chronicle delivered... she said they did; Shit!

I was informed, by the police, of a court date (so much for hearing no more about it) and it was only then that I thought about getting legal advice. I'd known Brad Stephens for years and knew that if anyone could help me he could. On the day of my trial, Brad stood up in front of the magistrates holding a copy of the "Cocaine Cannell" Chronicle aloft asking the bench "has my client not been castigated enough?" The magistrates agreed and fined me only one hundred pounds for the possession of a class A drug. Seemingly, I found out later, after analysis, the cocaine that the police had taken from me had contained so little of the drug that, had I not said that I thought it was cocaine, the case would have had to be scrapped! On leaving the courtroom, I jokingly said to Brad "do you think I should put my coat over my face like they do on the telly?" well I should have because, as I stepped onto the street outside the court building, this young lad took me photo then he legged it towards Pilgrim Street. The images appeared that night on both local news programmes.

I continued to publish hotel magazines then branched out into quiz books and a pub newspaper called Cheers until a chance encounter with someone who was to become a great friend. I'd met Ken Somerville a few years earlier in Pier 69, a pub on Newcastle's quayside, where he'd sent me over a bottle of champagne for no other reason than he was being Ken Somerville! I hadn't seen or spoken to him for ages when I bumped into him in my local pub which was, at the time, The Mill Stone; he was with his friend John Price. As I hadn't spoken to him since my cocaine fiasco, we had plenty to talk and laugh about over several pints and as many trips to the toilets! In the following weeks we continued drinking together as Ken had as much spare time as I did; the publishing game was getting tougher cos' the breweries were spending less and less on advertising and that was my main source of revenue.

One day, Ken, me and Alan Warman, another mate who ran a pub restoration and building company called Superior Interiors, were driving in Kenton when we passed a run down, boarded up pub called the Hawthorn. Seemingly an ex copper used to run it as a Vaux tenant but he gave it up as it was too rough for him to handle! It had been on the market for over a year with no interest at all. We all agreed that it had tremendous potential that hadn't been exploited. We also didn't have to worry about trouble with Ken and his brother John on board! "Give Vaux a buzz" Ken said to me excitedly "see how much they want for it." I called an ex colleague in the free trade department at Vaux and asked him what he knew about the pub; the story was a familiar one. They wanted a quarter of a million quid for the site, freehold, which was absolutely potty, however he also added that it was costing Vaux three hundred quid a week to pay a security company, to ensure the place wasn't taken over by squatters or vandalised. I explained all this to Ken, John and Alan and we all decided to put a bid in to Vaux for fifty grand, just to see what they'd say. I drove over to Sunderland the following day, to the headquarters of Vaux and made my way to the tenancy and estates department. Considering some of the dodgy deals I'd been involved in whilst working for Vaux, I was surprisingly warmly welcomed. I explained our interest in the pub but that we would only be prepared to pay fifty grand for it. They didn't seem too keen on the idea but they agreed to think it over. They said that they would contact me if they had owt' positive to tell me. I drove back to Kenton and explained the situation to the lads.

The following day, I received a surprise phone call from Vaux informing us that our offer had been put to Frank Nicholson, the boss's son, and it had been accepted as long as they received the money within twenty four hours. We decided to call them back and ask them if they would accept an initial ten grand deposit and the balance within two days (why we came out with that time scale I've no fuckin' idea, we still didn't have fifty grand!) Vaux agreed. Ken, John, Alan and I got together at the snooker club that John owned to discuss the situation or, should I say to work out how to come up with the dosh. We could get hold of the ten grand deposit, mainly thanks to John, but how could we come up with the balance within two days? The deposit was paid to Vaux and we promised the balance would follow once a nonexistent cheque had cleared (technically a porky!) Then Alan had a rare brainwave. He was good friends with and did a lot of work for Nigel Vaulkard who owned some terrific bars around the North East; he had a feeling that Nigel would lend us the money as he was also good friends with Ken and John. I also knew Nigel but it was mainly in my capacity as a free trade rep. I had been trying to get my products into his pubs for ages but to no avail; he always politely told me to "bugger off" as he said he couldn't give the stuff away! Anyhoo, Nigel came up trumps and said he would lend us the money which was a great gesture by a smashin' bloke who loved a pint possibly even more than Ken and I. Our next job was to head on down to the Mackem brewery to buy what was to become The Edgefield Lodge Hotel.

FUCKIN' HELL IT'S PAUL CANNELL

Once we'd bought the pub, we had to decide what to do with it. Although we all had our ideas, it was mostly down to Ken and John as they were going to do most of the work. John was only happy when he was knocking down walls, it didn't matter whether it was load bearing or not, down they came! He was and still is as strong as an ox; I'll never forget him holding a huge R.S.J. (a big metal girder) above his head, waiting for it to be fixed into place. There was all this work going on but all the materials and wages were being paid for out of John and Ken's pockets and Alan's credit with building suppliers. By the time the pub was completed, we needed to borrow around a hundred and fifty grand! I decided not to go to Vaux or Dryborough's for it. Enter Alan Newton, the area manager for Courage. I had known Alan for years as he used to work for Scottish & Newcastle Breweries at the same time as I had worked for Vaux doing the same job as me. He immediately realised that the pub would sell enough beer to qualify for the loan and so, within a few weeks, the funds were deposited in our bank. It was decided that since I had the most brewery experience I should manage the pub... which I did for some eight years until Alan and I, being short of cash as usual, sold our shares in the pub to Ken and John. There was no falling out or anything; anyway, you couldn't fall out with them, they would do owt' for you. I've always said that if I were kidnapped in somewhere like Somalia, I'd ring Ken or John before the British consulate!

During the years running the Lodge I had a relationship behind Linda's back with a woman called Audrey. It all eventually came to a head when her husband found out about us. When he confronted her about it, she immediately telephoned my wife Linda and told her about me and her; don't you just love fuckin' woman! Well that was that, it was a genuine black bin liner out of the bedroom window job and onto the front garden. After much too- ing and fro-ing, Audrey and I eventually went on to run The New Angel Hotel, a hotel, fun pub and nightclub in Whitby. This came about because Michael Quadrini's son Nicholas was going out with Dawn, Audrey's daughter and Michael owned the The New Angel Hotel. I actually knew Michael from my days playing for the Toon, when he owned The Tuxedo Princess and Tuxedo Junction which were the top nightspots in Newcastle.

We ran The Angel for a few years but it was only a matter of time before we eventually split up. I headed back to Newcastle to run another of Quaddies nightspots, Pier 39 and Breeze which were actually on South Parade, Whitley Bay. It was good to be back in the North East as it meant I was closer to my two smashing kids, Ally and Ross. Mind you I don't think they were that happy about my relocation... they enjoyed coming down to visit me in Whitby. I still don't see them as often as I should, but I hope they know that I love them and they always know where to find me. Linda and her partner Chris have done a great job bringing them up .Unfortunately Michael's company, Absolute Leisure, hit hard times and had to sell Pier 39 and Breeze to a Stockton based Leisure Company. They were obliged to keep me on but the job was never the same; the pubs had always been a pleasure to run under Michael and his ex missus Sheila who always considered the Whitley Bay venues her "babies" and so, with them both gone, I couldn't wait to get out.

THE BIG 'A'

Audrey's daughter Dawn was still seeing Nicholas Quadrini so I had stayed in touch with her throughout my time in Whitley Bay. When I read an advertisement in a local paper looking for management couples to run Spirit Group pubs in the North East, I got in touch with her to see if she was interested; not so much as a romantic couple, but as a business partnership. Within a couple of months we were running The Duke of Wellington public house which was a stone's throw from the Edgefield Lodge and also from where Audrey's ex husband lived. I spent a couple of the most miserable years of my life running the

FUCKIN' HELL IT'S PAUL CANNELL

Duke and I was more than happy to leave, or was I pushed? Anyway, that was finally the end of my relationship with Audrey! Once again I was jobless and skint. I had always kept in touch with Ken and John, Ken mostly, as John never touched alcohol; in fact the only thing John and I had in common was football. Some years earlier, we had run a West End Boys Club football team. We had taken a team from the under 8 age group, right through to the under 16 age group, winning trophies and plaudits along the way. John had spent a fuckin' fortune on them, taking them on trips, paying for strips and even buying their football boots if their parents couldn't afford them. Unfortunately it all came to an end when John had to spend some time at her Majesty's pleasure in some crap hotel in Durham; it was so bad they wouldn't let him out! I tried to keep the team going; I was o.k. with the coaching and training, but I was crap at organising pitches, referees etc. So the team we had built up from scratch folded. Ken had totally no interest in football, which is probably why we got on so well. One day I was drinking with him on Gosforth High Street when he chucked an Evening Chronicle at me pointing to an advertisement for a nightclub manager to run a new nightclub in Whitley Bay called "Heat" I went for two interviews, the first with a prat called Ian Sinclair who asked me how I would promote a new nightclub opening in two weeks. I told him I wouldn't because if you hadn't got plans in place by now, it was too fuckin' late! I got up and walked out. I was amazed to receive a phone call the following day inviting me to attend a second interview at the Park Hotel Tynemouth, with the club's owner, an Indian gentleman called Mr. Gill who also owned the Park Hotel, and his advisor Douglas Pearson. At this second interview, they explained that they had been impressed by Sinclair's report after the initial interview and basically, they wanted to offer me the job...if I would take it. It was that easy, so easy in fact, that most people would have been suspicious, except me! Anyway, I had no job and no cash so I thought "what the hell" and accepted the post. I arranged to meet Douglas Pearson on Monday, my first day at work. Heat nightclub had been built on the site of the old Idol's club which was, in fact, part of the Esplanade Hotel, at a cost of just under half a million quid.

Douglas was standing with Catherine, a receptionist at both the Esplanade and the Park hotel, when I arrived. This job sharing was very popular with Mr. Gill as I was soon to discover. Pearson explained that I wasn't exactly going to be managing Heat nightclub because it had opened already in order to catch the Bank Holiday trade; I was going to manage the Esplanade Hotel and oversee the running of Heat. The hotel had had no management for several weeks as the previous manageress, had been put in prison for selling cocaine to hotel guests! I felt right at home! Pearson took me on a tour of the premises, which was a real eye opener. There were mountains of dirty laundry piled up against emergency exits, televisions lying in the corridors, fire exits padlocked and a beer cellar that hadn't been cleaned since the war; I'm not sure which war. But worse was still to come. After he'd apologised for the hotel's shortcomings, as we were coming down the stairs towards reception; I ran my hand down the banister and 'came' into contact with a discarded, used, condom that had obviously been missed by the cleaners who, I was to discover later, were fuckin' useless. This was the reason they needed a manager I was told. Roll on Tuesday!!!

THE INFAMOUS ESPLANADE HOTEL

Anyhoo, I officially started managing the hotel on the Tuesday and that is when I met Yvonne, another receptionist at both the Esplanade and the Park hotels. We got on like a house on fire. She was gorgeous, loved music and was great fun. She and Cath explained that I had taken on the job from hell. I was then introduced to Neil (or Nellie as he was affectionately known) who was the hotel's chef. I had already been warned about his heavy drinking by Douglas Pearson. That to me was not a problem, the best chefs are either gay or alcoholics but the best chefs are gay alcoholics! The four of us were to run this fifty five room hotel that specialised in stag parties, hen parties and coach parties but Cath and Yvonne also had to work in the Park Hotel. There had to be someone on reception from eight a.m. until eleven p.m., drinks had to be available from the bar that doubled as the hotel reception and food had to be served in the restaurant for coach parties of up to one hundred and twenty two people. Oh... the restaurant had an a la carte menu available to non residents as well as serving Sunday lunches!!!

Nellie was a superb chef but no wonder he had taken to the drink working in this chaos. It only took me a couple of days to join him. The coach parties were the worst, especially when they all descended on the restaurant at the same time fully expecting an organised, high quality, three course set dinner. After a day of complaining about the hotels dirty rooms, televisions not working, showers hanging off the walls and a heating system that had a mind of its own; it was the least they could expect! One particular coach party stands out in my mind. They'd had the day set aside to explore Whitley Bay but the weather had been terrible; torrential rain and twelve foot waves breaking over the promenade in front of the hotel meant that most of the party had hung around the hotel, bored out of their minds. When six thirty in the evening came around they all made their way en masse to the hotel's restaurant. Yvonne skilfully managed to fit over sixty people into a room with only fifty chairs, the hotel's low window sills came in very handy at times. This party were due to stay for three days and so they had been given three evening meal menu selections on their arrival. Unfortunately these menu selections had gotten mixed up; Nellie had prepared the guests selections from menu two but the guests were expecting their selection from menu one! When poor Yvonne went into the kitchen asking for twenty four Northumbrian Turkey's Nellie hit the roof. "There's no fuckin' turkey Northumbrian or fuckin' Bernard Matthews... that's tomorrow" he bellowed "I've got fuckin' cod and chips or fuckin' pork... Now get your skinny arse out there and sort it out and get me a pint of fuckin' lager pronto!" The punters in the restaurant heard every word! How Yvonne placated the guests, who were baying for blood, as well as Nellie (well I know how she placated Nellie, continuous pints of lager) I'll never know; but she managed it.

The rest of their stay was just as bad; complaint after complaint after complaint. Even the bus driver, who had been looked after like royalty, said it was the worst trip he'd ever been on! On the morning of their departure I was just glad to see the back of them but Yvonne, being the trouper she is, decided to get onto their bus and wish them bon voyage. Catherine, Nellie and I just hid behind reception fearing for her safety. She told us that she had grabbed the microphone from the driver and then announced to the party "Hands up all of you who've had a good time". Seemingly, they all looked at each other in disbelief then, after some thirty seconds of stony silence, a sporadic ripple of applause broke out throughout the bus. The coach driver kindly whispered in Yvonne's ear "I'd quit when you're ahead me luv" then gently took the microphone from her hand.

Another source of complaint was the noise from Heat nightclub which was situated right under the hotel bedrooms. It didn't take a genius to work out that the thumping bass beat in the music would reverberate throughout the hotel. We were sick of explaining to guests "not to worry, the nightclub closes at two in the morning!"

After I'd had numerous confrontations with the hotel owners it was decided we'd go our separate ways. Not so Yvonne and I, I moved out of the Esplanade hotel and into her North Shields flat. She continued to work at The Esplanade and The Park for a couple of months until she injured her back moving beds from room to room and was forced to quit.

We were now both without a job and spent a lot of time in a pub, a mere twenty yards from where we lived, called the Alexandra. It was run by a feisty woman called Angela. We grew to love the pub and when Angela told us that she wanted to sell up we decided we'd love to buy it. It wasn't that simple however; my mother was living alone and showing growing signs of Parkinson's disease. We used to visit her four or five times a week and sometimes twice a day which was awkward as she lived in High Heaton and we lived in North Shields, some eight miles away. We decided it would be best for me mother to sell her flat and use the proceeds, along with our money, to buy the Alexandra. We'd then move me mother in with us and we'd become her carers cos' Yvonne had a background in care homes. Things went well for the first couple of months until my mother's condition worsened. We also started having problems with Enterprise Inns, the landlords of the pub. Eventually my mother had to be taken into an old people's home and the problems with Enterprise escalated; it really pissed me off that I could buy a keg of lager, from a beer company down the road over a hundred quid cheaper than I was forced to pay Enterprise. But that is what a brewery tie is … daylight robbery!!! Eventually we told Enterprise to stuff their pub and handed the keys back to their snotty area manager. Yvonne, Adam (her son), Louis our big, daft, black, standard poodle and I moved into a flat just up the road from the pub. It was great to get away from the continual hassle of running a pub, but we did miss some of the regulars such as Kane alias M.C. Ruption and his posse, John the roofer, old Alan and his domino gang, Ken and John who sat at the end of the bar bickering with each other continually but were really the best of mates, Keith the source of all knowledge (I hope he eventually wins the quiz jackpot) and the infamous Eddie the Eyebrow the Carlsberg Special King who some of the more stuck up regulars always wanted to bar…you'd think it was their fuckin' pub! Then there was Sammy, Sammy Laidler. When we first started drinking in the Alex, Sammy was THE barmaid…and what a barmaid! She was glamorous, hard working and the life and soul of any party. When we took over the pub we almost insisted she came with the fixtures and fittings! She became a great pal of Yvonne and meself and her son, Jordan, just happens to be a really good footballer…so much so that he has signed professional forms for ….wait for it… the Mackems!

Another thing we really miss is running the pub quiz. Some of the teams contained some real characters and many of their answers to the questions were hilarious; for example:

Q. Which movie featured the song "Always look on the bright side of life "
A. SCHINDLER'S LIST.

Of course the real answer should have been The Life of Brian……
Fuckin' magic!

So here I am sitting writing this book, it's four in the morning, Yvonne and Adam are asleep, Louis wants to go for a walk and Daniel, Yvonne's eldest son, the computer wizard, is working the nightshift at Nissan whilst his daughter Ruby is hopefully sound asleep. In the morning I'll be visiting me mother at the old people's home and Yvonne will be going to see her mother Kathy who is just gettin' over losing her husband of over forty years Davy. I wish I'd known Davy longer, he was a real character; he knew everyone in Shields and everyone knew him. When I was setting off to visit America to do some research for this book, Davy asked me, dead seriously "Aye, it's arl very well gannin' tiv America but d'ya kna' how to get there?"…… Pure Geordie genius!!!

Oh well… Life goes on…and as I drink me tea from me favourite mug which me mother bought uz some years ago, I look at the words enamelled on it
"OLD FOOTBALLERS' NEVER DIE, THEY JUST GO OFFSIDE!"

STATISTICS

Paul Cannell Appearances/Goals

Years	Team	Appearances	Goals
1971-2	England Schoolboys	3	3
1972-8	Newcastle United	69 (2 as sub)	19
1976	Washington Diplomats [on loan]	21	13
1978-9	Washington Diplomats	47	24
1980	Memphis Rogues /Calgary Boomers	28	7
1980-1	Detroit Express	5	1
1981	Washington Diplomats	13	1
1981-83	Mansfield Town	30	4
1983-4	Berwick Rangers	14	4

P.S. I'd better hurry up and finish this book cos' in the time it's taken me to write it, me mother's died, Georgio Chanaglia has died and half the world has participated in the Arab Spring!

We've just returned from a visit to the States doin' the tourist bit but also doin' some 'memory lubrication.' One night, I left Yvonne and her son Adam alone in the Americana Hotel in D.C. (which I would recommend, don't let the exterior put you off) where we were stayin' whilst I met Tony Quinn, Jimmy Finley and his lovely wife Dorrit downtown in the Black Rooster. When I returned she was laughing hysterically.. Seemingly, the take away I'd ordered them had arrived and she had asked Adam if he'd like some buffalo wings. As he was tuckin' in, she asked him if he was enjoying them. "Yes" he replied, "I've never had buffalo before." "They're chicken Adam" she explained. "Oh" said Adam "I thought they tasted like some kind of poultry. I thought that buffalo would be a bit tougher." He really is clever …honest!

FUCKIN' HELL IT'S PAUL CANNELL

Yvonne brought some fridge magnets back for her mother Kathy and for her auntie Jean. Fuck knows why, co's they've got that many already that every time I go for a beer I get a M.R.I. scan!!! When I was at Jean's, I asked her to do a bit of proof reading for uz...which she kindly did; she also suggested I should add a translation page...explaining what some of the Geordie words mean.

I agreed that it was a good idea and I thought that while I was at it, I'd add a page or two about some of the people I've met that I have a great deal of time for and also those who I have had some great times with, who I haven't mentioned in the book...so here goes...

GEORDIE	QUEEN'S ENGLISH
Fuck Kna's	*I really do not know*
Cos'	*because*
Me	*my*
Divvn't	*Do not*
Why aye	*Most certainly*
Crap	*pooh, excrement*
Mackems	*pooh, excrement*
	Only jokin', someone from the Sunderland area
Gizz	*give me*
Canny	*really nice or careful*
Gannin'	*going*
Twat	*Jimmy Hill*
Lass	*female*
Mate	*friend*

SPECIALPEOPLE

Jimmy Finley, Paul O'Sullivan and Finnegan aka Animal
Three bartenders from the Sign O' the Whale who I spent a hell of a lot of time with and who looked after me... in my rare moments of inebriation!

Mike O'Harro
Owner of Tramps nightclub and founder of the Champions bar chain. A smashin' bloke who inspired me to get into the pub game. Unfortunately I,unlike him, continued to drink as though I was a punter and not an owner! I will never forget his motto..." Poverty Sucks"

Linda Roth
A great girl who worked with Mike O'Harro in Tramps. I suppose you could say we dated for a while but we were really more good mates. She really helped me get used to the D.C. lifestyle. She and one of her mates would often come and tidy up my condo… I had two of the best lookin' cleaners in the U.S.A.! I hear she's doin', really well with her P.R. business

Nigel Robinson
A really good mate and an even better solicitor; he's pulled me out of the shit more times than I can remember. 'Robinson- Murphy', remember the name, you'll be in good hands. Maybe I should have asked him what he was like with Libel Law!

Teresa Fiduccia
A lass from my days in Memphis. She often drove me home in me Vette when I didn't even know I had a car! Teresa supplied me with the newspaper clipping of me and Stetz getting arrested after the Who concert. Why did she keep it? That's what's called 'remembering the good times.' Thanks Teresa.

Tommy Keeley
Tommy had a great club in D.C. called Cagney's. He was a Scouser who had lost none of his accent and I doubt if he ever will! He looked after us well! I can forgive him for bein' a Scouse.

John Gibson
Mr Newcastle United. He's reported on the Toon for as long as I can remember. One of the few reporters that the players trusted. He's forgotten more about the Toon than most journalists will ever know. He's been tryin' to retire for years… but it'll never happen!

SPECIAL THANKS TO
Johnny from the Product Agency, Mick from The Back Page, Jean Wilson and all the Newcastle, Washington and Memphis fans that made my playing days such a memorable experience. If I've missed anyone out… my humble apologies!

Made in the USA
Middletown, DE
17 November 2015